A WOMAN'S JOURNEY TO EMPOWERMENT

Written By Tammie Pike, Nicolle Edwards, Nyree Johnson,
Monica Alfing, Alane Millions, Christine Farnham, Georgia Hansen,
Lisa Foggon, Robyn Ellerbock, Louise O'Reilly, Carmen Smith,
Vanesa Gonzalez-Quinones, Joergette Mae Medel, Radhika Chugh
And Bek Tomarchio

Disclaimer:

This book is sold with the understanding that the authors are not offering specific personal advice to the reader. For professional advice, seek the services of a suitable, qualified practitioner. The author disclaims any responsibility for liability, loss or risk, personal or otherwise, that happens as a consequence of the use and application of any of the contents of this book.

A Woman's Journey to Empowerment

© Tammie Pike 2021

ISBN: 978-0-6453808-0-4 (Paperback)
         978-0-6451849-1-4 (eBook)

 A catalogue record for this book is available from the National Library of Australia

Editors: Melanie Lawrence and Janelle Shields
Printed in Australia
Published by Tammie Pike

EMPOWERED
PUBLISHING
Empowering Women to Empower

ACKNOWLEDGEMENT TO COUNTRY

Empowered Publishing acknowledges the traditional custodians of the land of the Barunggam people where this book was compiled. We also acknowledge all Australian Aboriginal and Torres Strait Islander peoples of this nation. We acknowledge the traditional custodians of the lands on which our company is located and where we conduct our business. We pay our respects to ancestors and Elders, past and present.

Empowered Publishing is committed to honouring Australian Aboriginal and Torres Strait Islander peoples' unique cultural and spiritual relationships to the land, waters, seas, and their rich contribution to society. A better understanding and respect for Aboriginal and Torres Strait Islander cultures develop an enriched appreciation of Australia's cultural heritage and can lead to reconciliation. This is essential to the maturity of Australia as a nation and fundamental to the development of Australian identity.

This book is dedicated to every woman who is willing to follow her heart, stand up for what she believes in, and trust in her ability to overcome life's challenges. Changing her world for the better, simply by being her true, untamed, and empowered self, therefore changing the world.

INTRODUCTION

"Our greatest ability as humans is not to change the world but to change ourselves. Be the change you want to see in the world."

- Mahatma Gandhi

At this very moment, it is a time of significant change within the world, and we are being invited to change with it. The old ways of being, the dictatorship, the censorship of yourself, hiding and staying small, are no longer. Have you felt it? Like your life is chafing at the edges and restlessness within your soul?

You aren't alone.

Like the women within these pages, millions of women worldwide are transforming and evolving, and their change is impacting their lives, families, community, and the world. Yet, like the butterfly, this evolution doesn't happen overnight. It takes time, energy, resourcefulness, and a whole lot of courage to allow the transformation to take place.

Old belief systems are crumbling, like a veil being lifted from the feminine as she rises from the ashes like a phoenix, where she no longer hides her truth, her needs, or her desires. She knows that by hiding herself, she denies the world the gift that her unique presence can give.

Have you ever been around a woman who has embarked on a journey of empowerment? A woman who has taken the time to understand herself and to heal? A woman who has invested in herself with time, energy, and money? A woman who has given herself permission to grow? A woman who isn't afraid to share her perspective and knowledge with others? Just being in her presence is healing. It's her energy and the bubble of love and magic she brings with her. Just like the butterfly, she instils awe and wonder wherever she goes without effort, without trying to please or be someone she's not.

This woman represents the women within these pages. You will see how they started at the caterpillar stage, and how they experienced trauma and challenges, and how they overcame their obstacles and used their experience and knowledge gained to fuel their strength, as they used their past to empower their future. They broke the cycle of those who came before them, everyday women who found the strength and the courage to keep growing, who were willing to change and change the world around them. They continued to step outside their comfort zone, becoming braver and more confident in themselves and their ability with each step.

Each woman shares with openness and vulnerability her struggles and, most importantly, how she overcame and rose up to create the life she loves. These women invite you to be curious in your own life, to be honest, self-responsible, and courageous in taking your power back. As their stories share, it wasn't an instantaneous change; it was years of making small decisions, investing in themselves, growing their self-love and self-belief to become women who own their life and chose to use their lived experiences to help others and to become authorities in their chosen fields.

These women wake up each day and continue to choose themselves and build a life that positively impacts those around them. It isn't easy; with each step forward, there are many steps backwards. Yet, their truth fuels their courage, knowing they have more people to support and empower.

This book is an invitation to you to take off the veil, to truly see your surroundings, and to be honest with your life, where you are at, and who and what you have around you. This is an invitation to accept where you are in this moment and to know that you are resilient and have the power to change it, and to take a step-by-step journey on your path to empowerment, knowing that it isn't your end destination, but rather a continual evolution.

This journey will require you to be kind, compassionate, and forgiving towards yourself, your past, and those within it. You must be willing to change, even though it can be scary when you and your world changes. But when you trust the process, when you believe that everything is working out for you, when you remember that, no matter what, you aren't alone, you will have the courage to stand up for what is right for you and those around you.

Take your time with each story. Let the medicine that each woman offers be a balm to your soul. And know that you only have to permit yourself to take the first step. I promise you that the universe will meet you and give you what you need. You might not see it to start with, but as your self-awareness grows, so too will your belief that you deserve to live a life you love, surrounded by people who love you for you. This life is your most precious gift. Don't live it with regret, in fear, or disempowered.

To get the most out of this book and the wealth of knowledge and skills, the authors have generously given freely, gifts of their knowledge, tools, and tips to experience and implement into your life. They give you these gifts in the hopes that it helps you somehow. Take the time to find them on their chosen platforms. See what else they offer you and the world. And, as you become a scientist of your life, allow yourself to be curious, to experiment and explore the practices they share, to see what works for you, and to make it your own.

There are a few rules on this journey - trust yourself. Be kind to yourself and those around you. Focus on how something feels rather than on how it looks. Be self-responsible. Seek support from others should you need it, including professionals, conventional or holistic. Be willing to receive and to become self-aware. And remember - you can't get it wrong!

After working with hundreds of women worldwide, the main issues that stop them from feeling empowered include fear and feeling unworthy. Fear - Many hide their truth, gifts, talents, points of view, creativeness, uniqueness (and so on) because they don't want to outshine others, be seen as a fraud, feel like an imposter, or have a fear of being visible, which is generally connected to past experiences. Feeling unworthy - Many do everything they can to not take up space or airtime (as I say) within their life or the lives of others, which means they spend most of their time trying to please everyone else around them, which means they are living their life for someone else. We know this as people-pleasing, and boy, do I know about that! I have had to work on creating boundaries and practising self-love and self-respect, like many women in this book who have experienced (yet overcome) by developing empowering practices. They also don't own their talents, achievements or experience due to never feeling worthy enough to be of value (in their minds) to others.

If you have felt any of the above, I want to tell you that, unfortunately, it's normal for many women to experience, and you are not alone. However, what I invite you to do is to no longer stay in that space. Be willing to release those limiting mindsets, fears, beliefs, toxic people, and situations by opening up to change and growth. To do this, there are many different techniques and practices that each author has shared, so don't sit idle as your life passes you by. Implement them. Find an accountability partner where you both support each other, especially when you get uncomfortable. Reach out to the women in the book and seek their support if they align with you and you can relate to their story. They have been there and may have gone through something similar to you, so they can understand what you are going through.

Please don't wait for a wake-up call that is so loud that it floors you. Listen to the whispers, small signs, and inner knowing that is already helping you awaken to your brilliance and power! Should you choose to listen, it will take you on a journey to empowerment.

FOREWORD

"Individually, we are one drop. Together, we are an ocean."

Ryunosuke Akutagawa

To the reader of this book, prepare to be invited into an inspired world. You will find yourself nurtured and supported as you traverse the pages like an acclaimed mountaineer. The highs, the lows, and everything shared in-between will help you to find the courage within your own life and to use a compassionate lens of self-love and empathy.

I am honoured to write this foreword, not only because I'm in awe of Tammie Pike and her many incredible successes, but as a woman's advocate, I share her passion for self-discovery and self-determination. I believe deeply in the educative and supportive value of creating platforms that enable women to connect with one another in an unapologetic manner that fosters growth and personal fulfilment. I also believe that, as women, we move through every stage of our lives and have a tremendous capacity to lean in, adapt, and thrive, regardless of the challenges thrown our way. By having the courage to learn and share our vulnerabilities with those who genuinely care, we have the capacity to heal and live the lives we desire.

A Woman's Journey to Empowerment is a compelling compilation of true stories brought to life by Tammie in a bid to share the wisdom and stories of a few to inspire many. Through her quest to galvanise and encourage, Tammie brings together women from all walks of life within these pages to inspire and nurture you as you face your personal voyage.

The challenges and hurdles that may have existed, continue to exist, or are yet to exist can be overwhelming and daunting when facing them alone. However, Ryunosuke's quote, "*Together, we are an ocean*" serves to remind us of the strength we have when we are united because it speaks to the power we hold when we bond together with great purpose. Regardless of our colour, religion, social demographic, education, or political affiliations, as women, we face many gender-based challenges. With the rising death tolls of women and children through domestic and family violence, never before has it been more imperative that we shake loose horizontal hostility and work to support each other. We must commit ourselves to ensure we use our individual and collective platforms to verbalise the issues affecting women both in our local community and abroad. *A Woman's journey to Empowerment* is where we all can start. As one, we have enormous potential to create better outcomes not only for each other and the ones we love but also for the most vulnerable in our community.

I hope you enjoy this incredible book as much as I enjoyed contributing to it.

Yours in service, reason and justice,

Nicolle

Nicolle Edwards | Founder and CEO | **RizeUp Australia** | (Pronouns: She/Her)

CONTENTS

Be Brave. Without bravery, you will never know the world as richly as it longs to be known. Without bravery, your life will remain small - Far smaller than you probably wanted your life to be"

~ Elizabeth Gilbert

NYREE JOHNSON

Nyree Johnson is an award-winning Central Queensland based small business owner passionate about business, women in business and her community. Nyree leverages her corporate career in parallel to her small business experience to connect with others, collaborate and celebrate successes.

Passionate about supporting her regional community, you'll find Nyree involved in many different organisations and causes across her region.

With an intense focus on empowering those around her, supporting her community, and demonstrating the benefits of diversity and equality, Nyree works to instil and inspire confidence, promote resilience and enable success now and into the future.

You'll find Nyree speaking, advocating, and writing to share her story, experiences, and knowledge with others. Her heart-driven tough-love approach as a small business owner sees her 'keep it real' regarding small business management and strategy.

Nyree is the creator of 'So you want to start a business', a simple and effective workbook to help you get clear on your objectives and goals. She has been featured in many print and digital publications, podcasts and interviews.

INTENTIONAL IMBALANCE

Motherhood, for most, is the deepest and most spiritually growing experience we will ever enter. After having children, a reality check set in and I quickly understood that my expectations were not going to match my reality. When you haven't yet experienced something in life, it is easy to daydream about what it will be like when it's your turn. And it's okay if our reality differs from our dreams and ideals.

My first child was born when I was 21 years old. I had spent seven blissful months at home with her before returning to work early due to financial obligations. As much as I loved my corporate role at the time, cutting my maternity leave short due to monetary reasons left me feeling like I was missing out and that I had no choice. I desperately wanted to stay home with my baby and dreamt of being a mum-at-home, daily.

When the Global Financial Crisis (GFC) hit Australia and the world in 2008, like most corporate organisations, mine commenced restructuring and reducing the workforce to come out the other side intact. At the time, two other people were fulfilling the same role as I was in the organisation. One of the impacts of the restructure was that these three roles were reduced to one, forcing efficiency in work and savings for the business. Thus, an opportunity for me to accept redundancy presented itself. As I was 16 weeks pregnant at the time, it was the perfect chance to resume my dream of having the ideal stay-at-home mum life with my toddler, while waiting for baby number two to arrive.

I enjoyed my time at home with my babies and was lucky enough to have enjoyed the privilege of spending a substantial portion of my days with my best friend, Christina. Our families were intertwined. Her friendship, love and support were the kind that comes along once in a lifetime. Christina was the type of friend you could easily spend all day with, and then speak to on the phone all night.

We were living in our state's capital city Brisbane, at the time. We were two years into parenthood, and my husband Nathan and I decided it was time to move back home to regional Queensland. We wanted to raise our family in the same town where we grew up. So, I said goodbye to my absolute best friend. We packed up our children and we landed at my dad and step-mum's home in Central Queensland. I was home. Nathan was dreaming of starting a career in mining, and I was planning to pursue a stay-at-home mum life.

With distractions aside — redundancy, pregnancy, new babies and moving towns — I began to find my feet in Central Queensland. However, I felt like something was missing. I missed the corporate life, my potential career and I desired something more. I was starting to realise that the stay-at-home-mum life wasn't for me, and that was okay. As much as I valued those early years of maternity leave and unemployment, I wanted to contribute to my community, connect with new friends, and have a fulfilling career that gave me something extra to celebrate. I also recognised that my children would be the single most amazing gift I would ever receive in this world. And in turn, they would be my legacy — me leaving this world a better place.

I began a journey to connect to my community and I managed to find a playgroup to join. The playgroup has since given me lifelong friends. I also became involved with The Cancer Council's Relay for Life. I participated in fundraising with teams for a couple of years before captaining my own team in memory of my grandmother Glenda Ross. She sadly passed away at age 68 from bowel cancer. Being involved in my community, albeit on a small scale, filled me with a sense of purpose and left me feeling like my contribution to the broader community mattered.

In addition to friendships forming and community involvement, I found a part-time position with a bank that offered school-hours work. I also successfully took on the role of treasurer of a local group my daughter was involved in. All of this, of course, happening in parallel. With Nathan in mining and his roster changing over the years through different variations, I was mostly parenting solo. However, I had fantastic family support and of course, Nathan's too, when he was home.

Our third child was born amidst this mining lifestyle. We spent three years in this space as a family of five. When our third child was almost a year old, an opportunity arose for me to return to the speciality career I'd left behind in Brisbane. I naively thought that the career field I loved so much, Workforce and Resource Planning and Analytics, was gone forever as opportunities were mainly overseas and in bigger cities. So, taking a chance, I left my secure bank position for a twelve-month contract role and returned to full-time work. This was challenging with a then one-year-old plus two additional children in primary school. However, I saw the long-term opportunity for my career and was prepared to make it all work. This, of course, added to the already full plate I was managing.

Discovering that our 10-year mining plan wasn't going to reach fruition at around the six-year mark, due to our growing dislike of the lifestyle, Nathan and

I began searching for an opportunity to bring him home. We started a mobile mechanical business with a plan to build the business on Nathan's days off from mining. Our goal was to reach the stage where he could return to our hometown permanently and be home every night with us. This endeavour kick-started my love of small business: marketing and advertising; business strategy and planning; providing regional job opportunities; training and development; and business financial literacy.

After two years of managing our mobile mechanical business, we purchased a brick-and-mortar mechanical workshop to add to the mix. This was the opportunity we had been working towards, and this bought Nathan home. Two businesses; a full-time career; various volunteer positions; plus mothering three beautiful children, had my workload at an all-time high.

People started asking me how I managed to fit so much in. How was it that there were more hours in my day than there appeared to be in anyone else's? Unbeknown to me, I had been practising an Intentional Imbalance. With additional committee roles I had taken on over the years in youth groups and local organisations, the workload kept growing. My ability to fit it all in was being crafted, fine-tuned, and my skills enhanced.

I'm not Superwoman and will never claim that title. However, what I involve myself in aligns with my values and brings joy to my heart. I know what I want in life, and I know how to achieve it. Having worked hard on clarity and self-awareness over the years, even when I feel lost or muddled, I know what it takes to pull myself out and keep moving forward. Strength, determination, discipline and resilience are traits I've developed due to life experiences. I've also inherited these traits from my family — raised to do good, be good and show up. It's not about being an overachiever or about overdoing it. It's about doing what you love and aligning yourself with what makes you happy and fulfilled.

I hope we all recognise that balance is bullshit. An Intentional Imbalance is a way of merging your roles and responsibilities. A philosophy to ensure you can do what you love and do what you need to. So, you can be involved with your own communities, groups or charities all at once. It requires an element of organisation and emotional intelligence, with some resilience and strength mixed into the equation as well. All of course, doesn't come naturally to most of us and requires focus and practice.

An Intentional Imbalance means you know which juggling balls are glass and can't be dropped, and which ones are made to bounce. Sometimes it means you need to hand over a glass juggling ball to a trusted person. For me, the glass ones are my children and my family, immediate and extended. An Intentional Imbalance means you can say Yes! to being you and Doing You. All while accommodating your other commitments, responsibilities and leveraging your skillset.

When I learnt about the Intentional Imbalance concept, I realised that was exactly what I'd been doing for years. I began researching the concept and started using the phrase as my default response when answering the frequent question: How do you do what you do?

I've spent years getting to know myself. This journey continues daily. It leads to a fantastic awareness of self and this world and how it all works, including the people in it. But, to achieve your daily dreams and your big dreams, you need to be disciplined and be willing to do the work to make it happen.

Dreams don't always have to be big, blue-sky thinking either. Daily objectives help keep you motivated and give you something to focus on with the added benefit of feeding the bigger dreams. Setting your intention for each day and capturing exactly what you will achieve ensures there is a structure in parallel to creativity. Being structured and organised doesn't need to look like diaries, to-do lists and calendars. It can be whatever works for you. You just need to unpack what that is. Remove the belief that structure and organisation will limit your creativity and flow, and recognise it as enabling your goals.

Self-discipline is the first step to self-love. Firstly, it is essential to have the right mindset to set yourself up for success. Yes, things go pear-shaped every now and then. But building your resilience-bucket daily means that when things aren't going to plan, you bounce back quicker.

For me, practising daily gratitude is the way I set my day up for success. By working through the following and spending five minutes completing this practice daily, you'll see a noticeable shift in your mindset. It helps to journal and write. However, this isn't for everyone and can be as simple as being mindful and thinking about each item. I must admit, though, it is more powerful written.

What is something that you are worried about that you need to let go of?

What are three things you're grateful for?

What are three things you need to focus on today?

At the end of most days, I also like to journal through my day's experiences and learnings. This practice aids with clarity and mindfulness and enhances restful sleep. However, it can be daunting at first when reflecting on the day and realising you flew through it without much thought. Still, this practice forces you to really take in what gifts the day gave you. It also helps you unpack any confusing aspects, by getting the words out of your head and onto paper.

Secondly, being prepared is vital. I always know what commitments I've got on for the day because I use a calendar application synchronised with my husband's calendar. We don't ask each other permission to attend events or accept invitations. If it's something we want to do and we're available, we simply check the calendar and add the event whether it be as a solo commitment or involving the whole family.

In addition to knowing where I need to be on any day, and who I need to meet with, I use a reminder application, on my iPhone, which captures my to-do list in order of date due. It is critical for my creativity that my headspace isn't bogged down with to-do lists and things I need to achieve. I capture them, add them to my list and schedule them for a day or time relevant and appropriate. I know most creatives shrivel at the thought of structure, but if this isn't your skillset, get a whiteboard or a notepad and draw it out. Moving things out of your head, from thoughts to plans and actions, enhances creativity and frees up headspace for more ideas, thoughts and opportunities.

Being on top of life doesn't have to be rigid and structured. You do need to find what works for you though, and stick to it! And, if you really struggle and your livelihood or dreams are dependent on it, outsource it to a friend, family member, assistant or even a virtual assistant who can set these strategies and organisational structures up for you.

Thirdly, know your values and what you stand for. This ensures that you only ever do what is aligned with your overall purpose and mission in life. It is common for this to be a mystery to people. I certainly know what that feels like. Asking yourself questions to get to know yourself through journaling may sound silly, but it is a practical way to find out what's inside your soul.

It's important too, not to place your own worth or value solely on a role, title, family or a group you're a part of. At the risk of sounding cliché, you are an amazing asset to this world and even if you don't believe in yourself, believe me until you work it out. Yes, this is also directed at the Negative Nancys, haters and online trolls. You're meant for bigger and better things.

Resilience and confidence are not always traits that come easily or naturally to us. Especially when we've faced adversity in our lives, or we've been torn down by people around us. I've found myself in undesirable situations throughout the years: manipulated; blackmailed; harassed and gaslit. So, I understand how challenging it is to come out the other side, or even to identify it when it happens to you. It can be a spiralling situation and extremely uncomfortable, leaving you to feel like there is no way out.

Suppose you've faced circumstances that have destroyed your self-confidence and worth. In that case, I beg you to work through this rather than bury your head in the sand or participate in self-sabotaging behaviours to numb the pain. Easier said than done, I know. This can be done in many ways. I urge you to be open to healing because when you're ready, the right path for you will present itself. Psychology is not the only solution here.

Throughout my life, I can hand-on-heart say that everything I've been through, from hurt to loss and love, has led me to where I am today. All of it has created the person I am. The same can be said about you and your experiences and trauma. The gift you have to share with the world is yours to actualise. You never know how impactful you are to the person next to you simply by being brave enough to share your story and experiences with others.

I've been blessed in life in that I have a wonderful, supportive immediate and extended family (flaws and all). None of us are perfect, but we're together, and we're there for each other. Likewise, I have a wonderful group of friends who keep me grounded, give me grief and cheer me on too. I too have been subjected to people who've come into my life purely to teach me lessons, bad ones at that, and I'm grateful for those as well.

Back yourself. You are here for a reason, and if you don't know what that reason is, that's okay. But plan to figure it out because the last thing you want to do is come to the end of your life with what-ifs.

Your definition of success will be different to everyone else, and that's all right. What works for you doesn't for others, and what works for others won't for you. Be true to yourself and focus on consistently showing up in the world. Each day strive to be better than yesterday. Set your intention and achieve. Don't strive for balance because achieving it is bullshit. Identify which are your glass juggling balls and which ones are made to bounce. Know your values and work on an Intentional Imbalance.

Please remember that when all the above goes to rubbish, and you're having a very average day or month - it's okay. So be kind to yourself and others. Know that you can try again tomorrow. Michelle Obama said, "Success isn't about how much money you make; it's about the difference you make in people's lives."

Your Gift

There are free downloadable resources, from setting your day up for success to reflecting on the day that was. You can find them at www.nyreejohnson.com.au .

MARILOU COOMBE

My journey to becoming an empowered woman began when I birthed into motherhood. It cracked me open in a way like nothing else. Living through war at a young age, going through a divorce in my 20s, living in five different countries before the age of 30 — none of that transformed me like growing, sustaining and birthing another life.

In my mid-20s, I was an au pair abroad and loved working with children. I was the baby whisperer for so many infants, yet when my first came along, I could not settle him in the way I did with others' babies. I felt like such a failure. I had such low confidence about everything I was doing. I trusted everyone else but myself. Heck, I trusted the sales assistant at baby buntings more than my intuition. I went through a dark time, emptying my cup, thinking that for my baby to be happy, I had to give him EVERYTHING.

While becoming a mother for the first time cracked me open, my second child helped me heal back together. I was more empowered and dictated what I experienced and told my support network what needed to be done. I wasn't afraid to be the expert on my body, my needs and that of my baby.

I learnt that I don't need permission to do what I think is best for my children. Whilst I listen to the experts, there is no better expert for my children than me! I finally learnt what it meant to be an empowered woman, which led me to be an empowered mother.

Marilou is a mother, coach and mentor, author & co-author, yoga teacher, workshop & retreat facilitator and youth worker. With a Bachelor in Social Science and several other qualifications, she is passionate about helping children and families live a highly purposeful life, instilling growth mindsets early on in life. Her mission is to empower the youth to have a strong self-belief stemming from their core.

MONICA ALFING

Monica Alfing is a Gold Medal Winner in fitness, an inspirational Public Speaker, a Goal Achieving and Balance Coach for Women, and a successful Meditation Teacher.

Monica is the Creator of Her Amazonian Health and Strength, a holistic business that works with the inner strength of women to help them with their purpose, goals and dreams in life, health, and business. She is known as a life-changing coach with a 100% success rate. She will be your biggest cheerleader and will dedicate her time and energy to getting you exactly where you want to be.

You can find her on YouTube and Insight Timer as a Meditation Teacher or Spotify with her podcast Mo-tivation. She has been a guest speaker at women orientated festivals and retreats, speaking alongside empowered women like Lisa Messenger and Gabby Bernstein. She has been featured in the Mumpreneur Magazine, local and international articles, magazines and newspapers.

When Monica is not training in fitness, she loves to go for walks, taking little adventures, and when she has time, she loves to be the barefoot hippie that she is and paint and listen to old music.

HER AMAZONIAN STRENGTH

I'd like to take you back to Wednesday 26 October 1994. It was a typical rainy morning in Autumn, during school holidays in a small town in the east of the Netherlands.

"Outside their family home, three young girls are running on the street in a state of despair, panic and confusion with no real idea of what is happening. Their socks are drenched from the rain; their hair is no different. It is no more than 10 degrees Celsius outside, but they feel neither the cold nor their soaking wet clothes. One of the girls is running towards the doctor's office across the street, then on to the end of the street, hoping to see the ambulance that the oldest girl has just called. The youngest girl had just received directions to run to their neighbour's house to get help. After notifying them, she races back through the garage, the house and into the hallway... and to a scene of her mum performing Cardio-Pulmonary Resuscitation (CPR) on her dad, who lays motionless on the cold white tiles.

She can see her mum, a former nurse, breathing into her dad's lungs with all the strength she can find while yelling "Come back... come on!" to her dear husband.

Frozen to the ground, the young girl suddenly hears her mum yell, "Go upstairs!" as she didn't want her young daughter of only ten to see what was unfolding.

Her father's skin is turning from yellow to blue. Finally, the ambulances arrived, from which the paramedics came rushing in. "Doctors!"- 'The heroes who make everything alright!" - as the girl's 10-year-old mind thought. The paramedics worked so hard, so hard to get her father back, they tried everything in their power.

Just on that particular rainy autumn day, day, their superpowers and those of her mum didn't work on her daddy. As on that day, her daddy died in that hallway, leaving his unforgettable imprint on so many hearts."

That 10-year-old girl, that was me. And my world, our family's world, as we knew it, changed forever on that day.

The day my dad died has been the origin of my dedication, strength and motivation for everything in my life. A massive heart attack, out of nowhere, was what took him from our world at the young age of 42. I learned quickly over the years that followed and through the stories of other young souls lost too soon, that life is short. I even started to believe that my own life would be short, and because of that, I started living.

Most of my personal growth came from my environment and from observing others live their lives. To pay it forward, I would like to take you back in time through my story to give you permission to think about your own story by first remembering everything you have learned, the lessons you gained and the strength you developed along the way. Not to focus on weaknesses or negativity, but rather the strengths. I know you may have been like me once. You may have looked at yourself and only found negativity, sorrow, a lack of self-love and a bunch of painful memories. However, as you dive a bit deeper, you will quickly learn that the story you have been telling yourself, is not necessarily the real story.

I will share more here about my practices and the lessons I have learned in my life. As I used to tell my stories in a negative, sad way, for that's how I was taught to look at things. Looking back through some of my memories across our family tree, I could now easily see how our family as a whole, shared the same dysfunctional perspective and were hard people to communicate with. They had a habit of always blaming others and consistently looking at life through a glass-half-empty lens. The negativity and sad stories have always been reflections and examples of what I had seen.

I started doing things and seeing things differently around my twenties, and so today, I want to share with you how I was able to break out of that cycle to change my mindset and how the Universe kept throwing various challenges to help me grow, so that the once young and broken girl I was, could turn into the strong woman I am today. At the end of the day, it doesn't matter what age you are; I now know you can always change your story.

In the years that followed our father's death, we grew quickly into teenagers and then into young adults, a lot came up. Alongside the stories in our minds of our parent's dysfunctional extended families and environments, we all created our own stories and our own lives. Getting more disconnected from each other over time, we began to hate each other, fight and created unnecessarily painful memories.

The louder our family home became, the quieter I became. I mostly just listened to the discord. I didn't go into discussion. I went out of my way to avoid conflict or trouble amongst my family. Days, months and years went by at our house, during which we learned how to get up straight away after falling, how to quickly wipe away our tears as if nothing hurt. We kept on going while licking our wounds in silence. It was as if I could see and hear all the goals and dreams of the lives around me coming, going, and dying in the house. Mostly due to blaming others or other random excuses. Strangely, the more I was exposed to the pain and disappointment, the more my faith and ambition grew within me. I had two choices: to believe and act the same as those around me, or to go the other way. I chose the second option.

From those times on, I began working on my life's purpose and passions. Including making beautiful memories, travelling and photographing life. I was only 15-years-young when I went on my first journey to South Africa, followed by Canada. This passion for travelling started out first as a coping mechanism to escape from the life I was stuck in, to have my own space and time to find my true self, passions and desires. Canada was where my dream of living in another country came true. Around that time, I slowly started practising living outside of my comfort zone. This led me to one of the best decisions I could have made in my life.

As a seventeen-year-old, with lingering shadows in my head, I started working in a nightclub. I started living and leaving my innocence behind. Years of fun, hard work and craziness followed — rock 'n roll, sex and alcohol. It was during this time that I developed a sort of strong confidence, sexuality and felt truly 'seen' for the first time. I have since returned many times to this natural inner strength I gained during this period. I felt like this force has always been there with me. However, through practice and action, I have come to believe in it more. This is also where my love and dedication for training and working out arose. Looking back over my life, when things got hard, or I was stressed, the one thing that always helped was exercise. Letting go and working the body to clear the mind. Some days I would walk, some days I felt like Forrest Gump running away from it all. Nowadays, exercise is my biggest non-negotiable of the day. Exercise is my healing practice. It has everything to do with the gift I want you to receive by the end of this story.

Now my story moves along to my twenties. We all remember those years, right? Trying to prove yourself; studying; working multiple jobs; stressing about money, and enduring broken relationships. I started two businesses in my twenties that gave me a lot of happiness, fun and a vibrant social life. It was one big cocktail of unneeded stress, sorrow, rock 'n roll and fast living. Then everything changed.

Early in my twenties, after just arriving in Melbourne as a backpacker, I was going down the escalators at the airport, where the weirdest thing happened to me. It wasn't the airport or the concrete walls nor the big tall buildings outside this city that did it for me. This was by far the first time I had really felt the Universe's power. This big force of power and light came over me. It filled me with happiness, belonging, warmth and overwhelm and said, "You are home." As simple as that, I had chosen the country of my dreams. This was going to be my new home! I lived with that dream daily for eight years after that moment. I began researching and saving money to move to Australia. I ignored the dream-crushers and non-believers — no one could have stopped me. Eight years later, I said goodbye to my friends and family, left a good life behind, full of memories. There I sat on the aeroplane for 25 hours on the way to Australia. With my hubby next to me, our two backpacks and loads of uncertainty and excitement. I had achieved my dream of moving to Australie!

Really, I can't leave my husband, my rock, out of this story. I had always thought of doing this dream alone, but instead, I had a wonderful man sitting right next to me on that plane that day to share the journey ahead...

I still remember when we reconnected two years prior, I was very honest with him and told him, "I like you and all, but I have a plan. Nothing can stop me." I explained that I always wanted to get married but I was also immigrating to Australia. The last thing I expected was for him to say yes and so quickly. Let's be honest who would do that in this day and age and after just one date? A year later we got married on a beautiful, private beach in Spain. I was happy, I was grateful, and I was in love. And to top it all off, I achieved my dream of moving to Australia!

Today as I write this, I am sipping my favourite tea and going to have an early night with a book. Tomorrow morning, I will start my day at 5 am with meditation, yoga and a big walk with my beautiful dogs. Later, I'll hit the gym in the afternoon, after I have enjoyed time with our beautiful two-year-old "rainbow" girl. I'm living the best version of myself with the daily practice of self-care and an inner belief that I can do anything. Let me share how I went from my lowest points in life, to winning a gold medal on the stage of a fitness competition, as a mum of a not-yet-two-year-old. Within my story, I'm hoping there will be inspiration and motivation to believe in yourself.

As the lowest point of my life wasn't so long ago, 2019, whilst in Australia and as a 34-year-old new mum, I found myself sitting next to my little daughter's bedroom door in tears. I was out of my bed for the dozenth time that evening, crying. In my arms was my crying baby girl. The child I had so desperately wanted for years. Years of pain I went through to have her; too many miscarriages, loss of trust in my body; all the unfairness. And there I was feeling guilty about missing my good old life? My first year of motherhood was nothing like I had suspected. A traumatic birth "broke" my body and I was in severe pain most days coupled with extreme sleep deprivation. I was filled with stress and feeling the pressure to be the do-it-all-mum. The pain of mastitis (blocked milk-ducts), a whole number of frustrations and feeling depressed, led me to despair. Add to that, the pressure of a toxic workplace that I was reliant on being employed into, due to the family visa my job granted us. I really didn't have a choice. This was the immigrant life I had chosen. The pressure was too much. That happy spontaneous girl with the big bright spirit slowly died before my own eyes. The fire inside of me was gone.

This overwhelming and low point in my life is what led me to my purpose — helping and coaching other women to achieve their biggest dreams, be that in health, life or business.

My personal journey of recovery was emotional, and it started by revisiting old belief systems and stories from my past, working through them one by one whilst physically moving my body throughout the process in a way that created the least amount of pain possible. I began going back in time and started telling my stories differently by taking full responsibility for everything that I went through. This is also where my passion for training and fitness helped as they gave me the clarity I desperately needed, they shifted my mindset and consequently working out has become a ritual just for me as part of my self-care routine.

There are so many women that are in need to break out of the cage they place themselves in. Not feeling worthy enough, or not knowing what to do next. Maybe burned out, stressed or unhappy. They feel lost and or like me, they lost their spirit. Having worked with so many different women, I know with self-belief, motivation and the practice of letting go, nothing is too big, and nothing is unachievable!

Together, I work with women to help them to start to believe in their inner Amazonian Strength, first with personalised practices. These teach them to start loving their bodies and minds again., as well as gain confidence to start changing their lives for the better. Including teaching how to gain happiness through the practice of meditation and mindfulness.

As women, we all have this old sacred Amazonian Strength inside each of us that we can use whenever we want. This is the source of the strength that will inspire you to create. It will motivate you to train; look after your body and mind; let you fight and that will let you love. It will challenge you to go deeper and conquer false beliefs, bad habits and help you take responsibility. This strength will leave you walking with glowing pride! It will let you feel as if you are a goddess and warrior in one!

I now use my journey to teach the women I work with. I teach that with determination and respect for their own desires, they can start to change how they look at themselves. I teach them how to stop using negative habits and behaviours and implement positivity. As a motivational speaker and coach, I show women how they can find their authentic selves, their purpose and create the life or business they authentically deserve. I only ask one thing of them; they need to be willing to commit to themselves and step off the edge of their comfort zone. That is where the secret of change lies. A bigger sort of happiness and love will start appearing in that space. A love you never want to leave — for yourself, your spirit, your dreams and your purpose. So, don't be afraid to find help or reach out. We all need a cheerleader sometimes (said with a wink).

The more you care about your life, health, body and mind, the more you will change your brain and energy. The world and environment around you will follow. You are a part of a bigger force. You are a woman, a goddess. Remember our ancient sisters; the witches and those who fought for our rights. You are forever a part of this Amazonian woman! You only have one amazing life to live. Stop pushing that "on-hold" button. The real change is within you.

Let this writing below be your present for the day. As it was created for you.

"And there she stands, at the top of her own created mountain. She has achieved the one thing she has always dreamed of. Standing tall and powerful as the sunset shines the last rays of her light on her beautiful skin. The reflection of her beauty shows in a tear of proudness on her cheek. Her Amazonian heart is open to all that she is, was and will become. She is a mother, getting strength from Mother Nature. She is a fighter, getting her skills from the always challenging environment around her. She takes care of her mind as she grounds herself with the earth beneath her. Her body image is impeccable as she knows she only has one body to take care of. One body that is so resilient and has never let her down, and so she respects it with all she has. She has scars on her body and soul, but she will never let anybody take her spirit. A fighter and an angel who nourishes and cares for all that she loves. She endured the storms that were needed, in order to conquer. She overcame the rains with the burning desire for sun and warmth. And while she stands here, in this beautiful sunset, looking over her mountains, over the seas of happiness, love, tears and beauty, she knows her power comes from all of this. From all she was, and all she needed to go through. It has always been her path. As her eyes pierce through you, she can see your true soul and you hear her whisper as a warm wind into the fire within you, "You are, and always have been a true warrior!"

This woman, she is you!

Now follow your ancient feminine instinct and go be who you were always meant to be. Start making thunder and create awesomeness with that great big inner Amazonian Strength of yours!"

Would you like to know more about Monica or know how to work with her? As a public speaker, you can find her online as a motivational and fitness gal that loves mediation, animals, family and friends. So, please reach out on social media, as she loves hearing her sisters' Amazonian stories!

Your Gift

And now... A gift is waiting for you: The official first: *You've got this girl!* - practice book. A practice book for changing habits; for movement; exercises; self-care; love and understanding yourself. Out of this practice book, growth and expansion can come. Embrace this with your whole spirit, as you are so worthy of being on top of that mountain you created!

Be the gift for yourself, much love from Monica.

www.heramazonianhealth.com

Insta: @monica_coachforwomen

Facebook: Monica Alfing or Coaching for Women

LIESEL ALBRECHT

Being an empowered woman means that I have choices in my life; I can say yes or no depending on what works for me. It means that I give myself permission to live a life of happiness and love and embrace those that give me joy, and fill my life with abundance and meaning.

It hasn't always been like this, and it has taken years to get to this point. There was a time where I was surrounded by family violence and continual worry about what would come next. With perseverance and self-discovery, it was a journey to get here. By reconnecting and remembering who I am at my core and in my essence has meant I can step into this position of empowerment where I have permission to be me whatever the setting or situation.

An empowered woman is walking on the path to be who she is meant to be and do what she is here to do.'

A woman, mother, daughter, sister, wife, dreamer, creator, nurturer and leader are all that Liesel Albrecht is and embodies in her everyday life. She has created an extraordinary business that whisks women into retreat settings where they get to reconnect and remember who they are.

www.lieselalbrecht.com

www.ultimategirlsweekaway.com

ALANE J MILLIONS

Alane (AJ) Millions is an EponaQuest (LLC) Horse Facilitated Learning Teacher with an extensive horse and human background, both nationally and internationally. Grounded in 30+ years of acquired skills as well as a depth of experiential learning, she facilitates the 'dance' between horse and human. AJ combines horse wisdom with common sense and has an absolute passion for supporting people to embrace horse wisdom. She delivers powerful, tangible and transformative programs while maintaining the integrity and wellbeing of the horse herd.

As a native Canadian, AJ was custodian of a 6,000-acre ranch with cattle and horses. She helped deliver horse programs in Okimaw Ohci Healing Lodge, a correctional facility for First Nations women. AJ has lived on the land of both New South Wales and Queensland, raising children, ostriches, emus, cattle, goats, sheep and horses. After co-owning a Wellbeing Centre for 6 years, AJ is sole proprietor of 'Leading the Way International'; supporting schools and at-risk youth on the Sunshine Coast since 2012 offering unique, tailored programs to people of all ages and abilities and welcomes anyone who holds an interest to co-exist amongst the herd and learn skills that will see them through their lives.

HEALING THROUGH HORSES

Empowered, strong women are born from adversity. I do not want to give anyone the assumption that the path to remembering who you are and embracing your power happens with a smear of meditation, a wall covered in affirmations and being able to downward dog.

Adversity and knowing how to navigate it, is how empowered humans are formed. It may not feel like it while you are wading through the quagmire of your lived experiences, however every time you pull yourself out of the bog, your armour is strengthened. I was born with a Kevlar armoured suit, passed down by the women before me. Amazingly, these were tough women who did not let their trauma define them. They never talked about their traumas, but they would pull me tightly into their bosoms as if their strengths were gifted to my soul.

I began to recognise their traumas after healing my own. It was then that I knew what an intergenerational, cellular mess they had to deal with, and had in turn, left me swimming in.

My mother did everything in her power to stop me from being abused. In the process of reliving her own story through me, she stripped my soul bare. It was through her beatings, making me wear humiliating clothing, the boy haircuts I was forced to have and her stopping me from having any male friends, that I was left feeling deeply confused and unloved.

It wasn't until adulthood that I was able to make any sense of her actions. Nothing was ever communicated, just anger and fear thrown at me like a punch to the stomach. I had no idea how to communicate with anyone, much less the opposite sex. Relationships were a struggle and I still find aspects of them challenging today.

While reflecting on my mostly "failed" relationships, the realisations of why I found them difficult became clear; this clarity came in a simple and complex number.

Twelve, twelve is my number. I counted the other day. I had to count after explaining to my partner why I ramp up and become defensive when the subject of sexual assault comes up. I allowed myself to search the recesses of my mind, tucked far away, the number of times from age 7 through 18 I had to fight off or get myself out of unwanted sexual situations with men. There are more situations I could count with boys my own age; however, they fall into the "they knew no better" category.

I never thought of myself as a victim when I was younger. I was known for being strong, resilient and a fighter. And fight, I could. I would stand up for anyone being picked on; I fought anyone who was mistreating others. I beat up boys until at least grade eight, and continued into early adulthood, fighting with anyone who pushed my various, deep buttons. Little did I know at the time, the fight I was having was to find my own damaged soul and to reclaim it.

From seven years old, I grew up on a 6,000-acre ranch in the southwest corner of Saskatchewan, Canada. The winters were long and unbearably cold, and life was about surviving. Summers were spent working hard to put up enough feed for the cattle to get through minus forty-degree winters. It was a perpetual cycle, year after year.

It was my maternal grandfather's ranch, and I was excited to move there as he had horses, a lot of horses. As far as I can remember back, all I wanted around me was horses, and my prayers came true. Life on the ranch was tough though, and as soon as I could handle chores, be it outside or inside, I was expected to work.

My grandfather and my mother had a volatile relationship. The intense anger between them was never talked about or resolved. They were both as stubborn as mules, and no one ever apologised. My grandfather was an alcoholic. Sometimes, I remember him having fun with us grandkids, but his drunken mean streak overshadowed those memories. Looking back at his life, it is no wonder. He was raised by a man who rode and shot buffalo with Buffalo Bill in the late 1800s. A tough man who, with his wife, raised seven children. If you weren't tough in those days, you did not survive.

I can still see my grandfather sitting in his wooden chair in the corner of his kitchen, knee crossed with felt lace-up boots, cigarette in one hand and a steaming cup of black coffee in the other. His brill-creamed hair slicked back, and fingers tainted by tobacco. The smoke from the rollie and dust particles danced in the sunbeams streaming through the greyish, smudged windows. His leg would be bouncing up and down slightly as he sat and contemplated the day ahead.

He was the kindest to me. I don't remember how he treated my brothers. His horses feared him, and the cattle experienced many hungry winter days, as his five-star whiskey addiction kept him well and truly occupied.

The stories from before my time did not paint a favoured picture. He would beat his wife, my grandmother, for sneaking out and giving the cows extra feed to get them through minus forty-degree nights. The neighbours were always helping her out with feed when he was on a bender in town with his whiskey-drinking cronies. Three little girls (my mother and her two younger sisters) grew up in a dirt-floored, two-roomed cabin with no running water and an open fire-place to detract from the iciness of the air and a father who had bitterness in his heart and iron in his hands. This is where the woman who raised me came from, born tough, heart shut down from cruelness and so found softness in the animals around her, horses in particular. My mother did not have an alcohol addiction. In fact, I can count on one hand how many times I saw her drinking. Her choice of addiction was anger and rage.

Myself on the other hand, I started drinking at nine. The whiskey that I had stolen from my grandfather's house was hidden in a glass jar down at the creek. When life got difficult and hard, which seemed to be often, I would spend hours watching muskrats and beavers swim by and drank the sadness away. Still to this day, I cannot believe that my mother did not know what I was up to. That tells me how poorly she was coping with the chaos in her life.

My mother and father had a turbulent relationship. There was a time it wasn't all bad, but when we moved to the ranch, life was never the same. My father seemed unhappy, pressured and a drinker. His sorrows were drowned in alcohol and anger, and he took it out on my mother. One day he left. It was a cold, snowy day, and my father drove off to a new life. His leaving set off a chain reaction I was not prepared for. His memories of those years seem watered down and diluted like ice melting in a whiskey glass. I wish I could have diluted them too and lord knows I tried, but the reality is, my parent's actions set me up to make choices based on my trauma for a good part of my life.

Did my father have regrets at that moment when he drove away? Did he cry as I did? I don't know. But 12 knows.

12 knows exactly what to look for; a young girl with no father for protection is like a baby fawn to a wolf. They can smell the innocence and sadness. They know that the fawn has no skills to protect itself, and they all know that the fawn has been abandoned. 12 was a constant in my early life, he appeared in many different forms. 12 was invited into my life, my house and they left a mark on my soul for many years.

I remember Mum having to hire 12 to help do chores and I had to fight 12 off and threaten to stab him with a pitchfork as he advanced on me while I was cleaning the barn.

12 was a teacher. 12 was my friend's father who pushed me up against the wall and started groping and trying to kiss me until I kneed him in the groin and ran. 12 was a man who stopped to help me fix the tractor when it broke down. 12 was the farmer who wanted me to leave my tractor to come and ride in his combine with him. 12 was a close relative who could not keep his hands to himself and grabbed a feel of whatever he wanted.

As my life unfolded and some stories were shared with friends, 12 was a frequent visitor to us all, and crept into our lives and affected how we saw the world and who we became. All of these adverse childhood experiences had deep, profound and cruel effects on my psyche.

I would like to say that I overcame all the adversities quickly and became a confident, self-assured woman overnight. However, we all know that is not the way life's trajectories are. I worked hard at being normal and having a normal life, marriage and two beautiful children but my past was preceding me and the effects it was having on how I saw the world affected every decision I made. My subconscious was controlling my mind. I was on a rollercoaster gaining speed and I was in for a traumatic, agonising free fall again.

I was 31 when my mother Mary and her little white dog, Pookie, went missing. She was travelling home late one night after visiting her mother. It was a two-hour drive on dark, dirt roads in the Saskatchewan prairie of central Canada. It was springtime; the grass was not yet green. Nights were still very cold. The cows had started calving, and being a rancher, Mary never stayed away from home for very long. I gathered my friends together, and we began searching. We found no clues. During the two-hour drive to the city, I retraced her path to the best of my ability. Nothing new was revealed. I felt my world starting to spin out of control. I would travel that long road, driving the four-hour round trip every day for twelve days. I told my friends, "I feel like I am driving right past her on the road, but I can't find her." I had never felt so helpless.

The small, local community was amazing. Kind folks organised searches on horseback, quad bikes and by car. The local Royal Canadian Mounted Police (RSMP) and other support people searched every conceivable road and abandoned building along the two-hundred-kilometre stretch—still nothing.

Days began to blur together. Air searches commenced, and the media had run with the story. Mum's disappearance was getting widespread publicity. People now had a face to go with the name and a photo of the vehicle. Surely this would yield some helpful information. Alas, still nothing.

By the tenth day, the collective spirit was wavering. The continuous, fruitless effort was taking its toll on everyone, and a dark cloud seemed to hover over our normally sprightly community. The police were considering the possibility of foul play, interviewing family and close friends. Being treated as a possible suspect in the disappearance of my own mother took me to a new low. I felt defeated.

On day thirteen of the search, the police called it quits. I was gutted. This was the lowest moment of my life. I relived everything I could remember – things I had said to my mother, especially during our final times together. I realised I had not hugged her goodbye when we last parted. I couldn't remember the last time I had told her that I loved her. I realised I might never again have the opportunity to tell her.

When the sun rose the following day, melting the frozen hills, nothing felt like it had changed. Normally, I would raise my face to greet the sun and feel the comforting warmth of the fresh morning. For me, there was no goodness in this morning.

I drove into town with my friend, Doug. He went to check in with the search team headquarters to see if there had been any developments overnight. The moment I spotted Doug approaching, I knew. He was telling me that I needed to go to the police station.

The local constable had received a fax from a woman who lived two hours east. She had heard about mum on the television and immediately felt intensely affected. She was the same age, and she listened intently to the story. That night, this woman dreamt about my mother. Information about my mother's situation came to her in her dream, in a cryptic fashion.

Upon waking, the woman wrote down everything she could recall from her dream. Using a map of the wider region, unfamiliar to her, she used the information in her dream to locate and then circle in pen the place on the map where she felt the police would find my missing mother. The information that seemed confusing to the woman, made perfect sense to locals who knew the area well. The map and the cryptic information from the woman's dream, led the RCMP officer to Mum's exact location.

Somehow, my mother had missed her turn, and the road she was travelling on ended suddenly, with no warning. Her truck had flown off the end of the road, landing upside down in a ravine. The coroner later confirmed she had died instantly.

Concealed at the bottom of a ravine, the camouflaged vehicle had eluded the intensive search by police and locals. Mum's faithful companion, Pookie, had somehow survived the crash. She had not left her side. She was dehydrated and nearly starved to death, but would eventually be all right.

My world as I knew it had ended; yet there was a certain amount of relief knowing my mother had not fallen prey to unsavoury people. At least I had answers to my questions. As I grieved over the next few months, I found ways of getting on with life: the ongoing responsibility of raising my two boys, and now, suddenly taking over full responsibility of our ranch. Luckily, I had been able to chat in-depth with the lady who had the dream. She told me this was not the first time she had received important, real-life information from a dream. In fact, she had lived with this incredible gift for as long as she could remember, and she had learned to trust it.

I had read about people like this in tabloid magazines but never gave them any merit. My belief in a higher power had waned over the years and I simply did not feel connected to a higher source. In this moment, I found myself completely reassessing my spiritual beliefs. My first-hand experience showed me directly that a higher power, a spiritual connection of Love does in fact exist.

I have come to realise that we must have faith in something bigger than ourselves; this faith supports us when times are tough. There is so much more to this world than we are able to perceive with our basic senses. We must remain open to people who have the courage to share from the heart, even when that sharing stretches the boundaries of what is accepted as normal or readily understood.

For me, my mother's dramatic death became her amazing way of waking me up to what is truly important in the time we have. Years down the road, life has led me on such an amazing journey of joy, faith and real magic. I get to "work" in real magic every day and feel blessed to be able to use my lived experiences and passions to support people from all walks of life. Learning horse wisdom helps them expand the quality of their lives. This wisdom kept me alive and evolving over the years and it is a privilege to share.

When I awake here in paradise, at my *Horse Facilitated Learning Centre,* I look out my window at the paddock of beautiful horses, and I know my mother gave me this incredible gift. I feel her with me often, she sends the eagles to visit and guide me. Her love and the occasional "kick up the butt" is felt from another realm.

Your Gift

In appreciation of you purchasing of this amazing book, Alane would like to offer you her Horse Meditation that will take you on a magical journey with a black horse. It will support you to relax your heart and soul to join the Horse Realm.

She would also like to offer you a Horse Card Wisdom. Each of our horses has wisdom that they offer to us. This Horse Card will come in a PDF for you to have to print out or save on your device. Simply email Alane at leadingthewayinternational@gmail.com with the subject Empowered Woman, and it will be sent to you.

The only thing that was ever wrong with me was my belief that there was something wrong with me.

~ Glennon Doyle

CHRISTINE FARNHAM

Christine is an Intuitive Mentor and Kun Yin Feminine Energy in Motion teacher residing on the divine coastline of Australia. Her energetic healing journey began after going through her own tough, painful stresses and traumas. She is motivated and inspired to support others in their journey to healing and happiness.

Christine sees what many don't. She has a very strong connection to the Universe/Creator and helps others heal and let go of what is no longer serving them. With Christine's help, rediscover what gives you passion and lights you up inside through energetic healing, meditation, essential oils, and movement.

NOT AGAIN - HOW I DISCOVERED MY TRUE FREEDOM AFTER A DIFFICULT RELATIONSHIP

Not again. These were the words I had whispered to myself over and over again. I had failed, and others had failed me, yet again. My anxiety was overwhelming. My distrust in myself and others was at an all-time high. I didn't feel safe, and I didn't feel loved, especially when it came to loving myself. How could I when I felt no one could love me in the way that my soul yearned for?

Another failed relationship had taken me to an all-time low. I can't remember the exact moment when I realised that my relationship had turned from loving to toxic. How had I ever let myself be treated with disrespect and be belittled for the slightest thing? It was so bad that I never knew when the next torrent of derogatory words would be flung at me, followed not long after with "I'm sorry and will never do it again". Until the next time. And there was always a next time. It was an emotionally draining relationship that left me feeling helpless, dead inside, and very alone.

Looking back, I see how I got lost within the expectations and duties of being someone's partner, a mother, and a woman. I ignored the signs because I didn't want to believe I was in a relationship with someone who would choose to hurt me emotionally. I made excuses and forgave, yet without realising it, I allowed another person to change me, and not for the better.

It's saddening that many people (including me) stay in situations that diminish our self-worth because we were never taught how to value or prioritise ourselves. Instead, we hide our not-so-perfect lives from the view of others in case they think less of us or our partners. I know I felt ashamed, stressed, alienated, and alone, yet I continued to stay, as each time something bad happened, it was followed by something good. It was the good parts that I held on to tightly. Unfortunately, these moments were rare and few and far between. I kept telling myself that things had to get better... right?

I know that many who are or were in a toxic relationship like the one I was in don't have support. However, I was fortunate that I had support. I had my parents and a girlfriend who would pick up the phone no matter when I called her. I don't remember how many times I rang her during those hard days. I recall always having to time it right when I rang her so that I could talk freely, without interruption and fear of being overheard as I vented about the latest incident. Another source of support came from Mums groups that also offered me a reprieve. These women were my saving grace, mentally. I ended up becoming a part of two circles of mums. These connections and commitments gave me a reason to leave the house and forced me to interact with others who would hold space for me. Not only did they allow me space to vent about the latest crap I was dealing with, but also to feel human and semi-relaxed for a couple of hours. They also gave my children a fun, relaxed environment to play in and just be kids, without tension around them. I didn't realise at the time how helpful it was to talk and get it all out. They helped me feel lighter and clearer in my mind, enabling me to take on whatever was to come next.

It took four attempts to finally leave that relationship. Its ending was my new beginning: the rediscovery of the woman I used to be, who was confident and outgoing, and who didn't care what anyone thought. I had owned my world once. I wanted to be her again.

The day I knew I had to end the relationship was the day I realised my situation was getting worse. Things were never going to get better. The last shred of hope I had for this relationship had completely vacated my body. It had left me as an empty vessel and I was left on autopilot to function. It was the day that I stood up for myself and told my partner I would no longer tolerate being treated with disrespect. He laughed at me and didn't believe I could or would leave him. Again, the taunts came thick and fast: "You've got nowhere to go. Who will have you? No one will want you. You're nothing without me!" I let his words rattle through my numb body. How would I do it? I let his words echo through my fear. I wondered to myself if I was indeed prepared to do the things I had to do, knowing it was going to be hard for everyone involved. Again, where would I go? I decided that if this was where I keep arriving at in my mind, then clearly this relationship wasn't going to work. How could this be a healthy environment?

Naturally, I had all kinds of emotions come up after I left. There was the shame and embarrassment of having a failed relationship. I was angry for allowing myself to become completely lost in something that was so toxic. It was a big, new chapter for me, too. I had to learn how to be a single, working mum, and to rediscover who I was. It was time to re-remember what lit me up and what excited me about life.

I've always been an intuitive person; I am very clairvoyant (I see things that others don't). Yet, I had managed to switch this gift off during my teen years. But when I was pregnant with my daughter it started to come back, and then I nurtured it more during my second pregnancy with my son. It felt good to do something that was just for me. It also gave me a sense of safety and something else I can't quite explain. To accommodate my family's needs, I had changed jobs a few times. It was during my last job in hospitality, that I allowed myself to follow, and really start to develop my intuition. I was intrigued to see where this 'big-calling' would take me. I completed my Reiki I Initiation course, and completely surrendered to what my soul knew had been residing within me all along. And so, I embarked on my new quest—a brand-new chapter of my life. So far, my life had been a roller-coaster of mixed emotions. However, nothing could have prepared me for what my self-discovery journey was about to bring.

When one completes their Reiki Initiation, they need to undertake 21-days of self-healing. It is also highly encouraged to practise your Reiki Healing on family members wherever possible during your training. So my kids lapped it up! I noticed that the more I did healing on myself, not only did I begin to feel calmer within myself, I began to trust my intuition more. With this trust, the connection with myself became stronger. Naturally, the more clarity I gained around what I would and would not tolerate transferred to my hospitality work.

What was I doing? I had left a relationship to start a better life. Why had I allowed myself to fall into the mindset of putting my family's needs second to others? I was working my arse off to provide a life for my children, yet I hardly saw them! I was juggling work, school and daycare drop-offs and pickups, and after school care runs. During school holidays, I would drive the interstate so my kids could spend time with family instead of being in holiday care, only to then turn around and get back to work the next day. I felt so much guilt around this. I hardly saw my kids and it sucked. Cue the mother's guilt.

I wanted to be there for my children. If they were sick, I wanted to be home with them without feeling bad for letting work down because they had no replacement staff. Or on the other hand, due to my employer having no relief staff, I needed to take my sick child to work with me. If they had an award ceremony at school, I wanted to be there, yet I didn't know how to say no to my work.

I realised without a doubt that things had to change, that I couldn't continue drowning in guilt the way I was, that I needed to spend more time with my kids guilt-free. Finally, the day came where the Universe opened my eyes with absolute clarity: I could make things work for the better! I didn't have to continue 'just being a number' in someone else's business. I was more than capable of helping others the way I wanted. I could create my own income as well as create the life for my family that I yearned for. And so, I began.

I took that huge leap of faith and decided to leave the safety net of mainstream work. I started my own business. Previously, I had qualified as a relaxation massage therapist. I just knew between that and my Reiki abilities, I could create a wonderful business where I could help others heal on many different levels of their being. Better yet, I could create my working hours around my children's needs.

After sharing this decision, I'll never forget someone asking me: "How will you make this happen? You have no clientele. No one knows of you yet. You have no guarantee of an income!" I just smiled and replied: "I have no idea. I just have absolute trust and faith that it will work. The Universe will provide for me." And guess what? It wasn't until I said these words out loud that I realised it was entirely true. That was during December 2015. On the day of the new moon in February 2016, my new business Eternal Lotus opened its doors to receive my first client. I have not looked back since.

The more I did Reiki on clients, the faster and stronger my intuition grew. And as my intuition grew, I realised there was so much to learn about how our emotional bodies hold onto trauma, pain, heartbreak, guilt, resentment, and similar feelings, and how those feelings, in turn, create physical issues in our bodies. I was then introduced to the ThetaHealing® technique.

Even now, writing these words, my heart skips a beat at the joy of having discovered this incredible healing modality. ThetaHealing® has completely transformed my life, and I dread to think where I would be without it. It was through using the ThetaHealing® technique that I was able to clear the mother's guilt, shame, and embarrassment I had been carrying since leaving the last relationship and bringing my children up as a single working mum. I had seen myself as a failure. But I was then able to clear so much resentment towards the men in my life who had hurt me. I hadn't realised how much I was still hurting. I was also able to discover generational beliefs that had been passed down through my ancestral lines, (due to certain circumstances), and was able to change them. This ThetaHealing® was powerful stuff! I felt that everyone needed to know how to do this for themselves. So, I now teach the ThetaHealing® technique to others.

Through these healing modalities along my path, I became stronger within myself. I learned how to love and nurture myself and to feel that it was okay to do so. The more I did this, the more in flow my family's lives became. The most important thing I learned, though, was how to put my ego aside and forgive. Not only others, but myself for being in certain situations. I forgave myself for doing something that I never thought I would ever do and for finding myself in difficult situations — I chose me, I prioritised me, and I chose a life I wanted to create for my children.

I have had many big lightbulb moments during my intuitive-healing journey. But one of the most powerful realisations I have come to is this; our children choose us to be their parents, just as you chose your parents before your mum birthed or adopted you. What did you learn from your upbringing? Did you have a traumatic upbringing? Was it the best childhood anyone could possibly imagine? What did you learn from it? Now think of this for your children, or a child that you know of. This may make you feel teary at first, but allow yourself to feel it. The most important thing to know is that no matter how shitty a situation is, it's an opportunity for growth. Now think of your children. How have they changed and grown? There may be times when you're questioning: 'What have I done? Why would I put my children through this?' Know that your children are growing within their own unique journey in their life. When I told this to a client, she cried at this realisation. Through her tears, she said: "So it's a privilege that my children choose both of us as their parents? Even though it can be hard at times?" Yes, it is. I still need to remind myself of this at times too.

I continue to grow each and every day. I have found the woman who loves life, is confident, and who owns her world. My life has included detours, yet with each detour and challenge, even though it wasn't what I wanted, I know it is exactly as it's meant to be, and each time I have grown more as a woman, by being committed to listening, honouring, and trusting myself and my intuition, just like I did when I knew I was going to be okay when I chose to leave a toxic relationship. Or when I knew that learning Reiki and ThetaHealing® would help me evolve. Just like when I knew that the next step for me was starting my own business. Each time, I have trusted my intuition, and it has allowed me to transform my life for the better.

So it's no surprise that I followed my intuition when I felt something was missing. It was the connection with myself, my body, and my femininity. I needed to get out of my head and into my body. It was time to embrace and embody me; that is when I found KunYin Feminine Energy in Motion.

I found that when we are focused on what is wrong in our lives, it reflects in our physical bodies. Your body is an incredible vessel that loves you and wants to do its very best for you - we each are walking miracles. Being caught up in your head can leave you feeling disconnected from your physical body. Sometimes, we disconnect to survive, so we can still 'function' and get through the day. Behaving like this can be common after experiencing trauma, abuse, or living in severe pain. By disconnecting, it means we don't feel.

I am speaking not only from an Intuitive Healer's perspective, but also from my personal experience. I was a master at disconnecting from my body. She was holding onto so much pain, trauma, abuse in all forms, grief, anger, and so much more. When my body was whispering to me that I had things that needed to be addressed, I ignored them. When the physical alignments got worse, (aka my body screaming at me), I completely disconnected from her and was just existing. I completely believed that my body had betrayed me; I was embarrassed and ashamed of my body.

Kun (Kundalini) Yin (Feminine) took me on a journey to re-remember how to connect me to my body. I learned how to listen to what my body is telling me. KunYin helps you get out of your head and drop into your body - including your heart space. It allows you to tune into your feelings whilst being guided by a teacher and supported by the music. It helps you drop out of your head and into your body, giving you the freedom to listen to how your body wants to move. It deepens your trust and intuition, as you start to listen to yourself more and more.

KunYin helped me to re-remember how to be me. The more classes I did, the more connection I had with my body and I rediscovered incredible wisdom. I discovered how my body needed to be loved and nurtured. I saw the memories my body was holding onto and why I had become so disconnected from her over time. I shifted what was ready to be released in a very different way than I had ever experienced. I remembered who I truly was, and discovered how to claim my True Self and show Her to the world. I fell in love with my body. I also gained clarity within my life, including my relationship with my body as well as others, and I haven't looked back. KunYin helped me so much that I became a KunYin teacher, and now I help other women connect with their bodies and wisdom. I truly believe every woman needs this in her life.

I wouldn't be who I am today without my experiences: the good, the bad, and the super ugly. I am most grateful to myself for having the courage to step out of a toxic environment and create a life for myself and my children that I could never have imagined. I am grateful that I continue to learn and grow to experience my life in a more empowered, exciting, and pleasurable way.

Do I still encounter trying situations? Yes.

Do I get triggered? Sometimes. Thankfully, though, not like I used to.

Now I invite you to take an honest look at your life. Are you concerned for you or your children's wellbeing? Are you feeling constantly on edge? Are you made to question yourself? Are you ridiculed for being you? Do you look back on your life and think: 'Who am I? What happened to me? How did I get here?' Do you feel trapped? What do you dream your life to be? How do you see your children growing up?

There is help. You're not alone. You have the power to create the life you choose. Are you ready to create change?

As every Empowered Woman knows, her journey is her own personal experience, and her story to share, not that of others. I share what has been my Journey to Empowerment in the hope that it inspires those who may need help, or courage, through their journey.

For more information on how energetic healing may help you please head to my website www.eternallotus.com.au

Your Gift

Christine has created a simple, yet effective, meditation to help you go within and find the true answers for yourself. Simply email Christine at christine@eternallotus.com.au and she will send you a link that contains a pdf and a pre-recorded guided meditation. Here you will be taken on a journey to discover clarity on the answers to the questions you seek.

Connect with Christine: *Eternal Lotus* is for training, energetic modality classes, meditation classes and dŌTERRA information at www.eternallotus.com.au

Facebook & Instagram: @ChristineFarnham8/

METTE SORENSEN

"Empowered" to me is "WE, not ME"!

I know if people believe in themselves, they'll amaze themselves with what they can accomplish. The more you know yourself, the greater your influence becomes in the world as you journey your chosen path.

I work mostly with social, educational and psychological empowerment and I have found that to maintain a state of empowerment takes a tribe. This means that you become accountable for your actions, time and energy as you give and receive support. To be empowered is to be aware of what you want, to know that the sky is your limit; be focused and mindful of where you wish to be. Most importantly is to be conscious of doing things that give you energy for your body and mind every day.

Practices that I use to help me are to speak the truth from the heart, prioritise every day by asking myself, "What do I need for me"? What can I do for my partner and then my team? This way I'm always in integrity and have taken care of myself so I can take care of others

Lastly, being an empowered woman means that I pass on my knowledge and support women in all walks of life to raise the vibration of self and others, which I love to do.

Author, Dynamic Retreat Facilitator and Teacher Of Kahuna Massage, Mette is a dynamic facilitator and teacher whose purpose is to inspire through the empowering qualities of teaching and provide tools to enhance people's wellbeing and those keen to enhance their skills in holding space and leading/facilitating change through integrating mind, body and spirit.

www.highspiritsretreat.com.au/

Georgia Hansen

Georgia Hansen is an eclectic mix of PR, marketing communications savvy, and intuitive wisdom with a deep understanding of human communication, collaboration, and connection.

She is an International Bestselling Author, Speaker, PR & Marketing Mentor who uses her voice and light to shine on and amplify the messages of extraordinary women who are ready to be seen and heard. She can see through the gaps as well as hold the vision for the bigger picture.

Georgia is an editor, writer and speaker. She has been featured on various podcasts, summits and events and published in Mumpreneur Movement Magazine, The Herald Sun, Courier Mail, News.com, EssentialBaby, Elephant Journal and HealthTimes.

She is a mother and an angel mama, with four of her babies residing earthside and one in heaven. She has a powerful story, message, and mission to shift a paradigm around loss, trauma, and tragedy. She teaches there is grace and magic to be found in it all.

FINDING YOUR GRACE THROUGH GRIEF

Imagine that within life, everything was happening for you. As part of a much bigger, grandiose plan. Imagine if even the most tragic, cataclysmic and life-altering event could also be the most sacred and magical. What if the deepest, most raw and painful moments of our lives could also bring forth our deepest sense of knowing? What if those moments lead us to find our *True North*, our power and our *Grace*?

As with everything in the Universe, we are made of energy first, matter second. We are like tiny particles of water in a gigantic ocean. We are specs of stardust in a cosmic explosion. We are all so small. Each of us is so much smaller than the *Great Whole* out there. There is something far bigger than us in our physical form as humans. I believe it is the *Infinite* that created us all. The Cosmos that houses us, or the benevolent Universe that is always working on our behalf.

I'll always remember the words of my best friend on the day of my daughter's funeral. Whilst her coffin was being carried out to the hearse by four solemn soldiers (my husband, his two sisters and their father), my friend turned to her mother standing beside her as a wave of rage suddenly pulsed through her veins, she blurted out, "Why is this happening? It's not fair!" Her mother, ever so wise, turned to my friend and calmly stated, "My darling, we are so small."

Something about this moment brings me straight back to *my* knowing. To *my* power and to who I truly am. To my *Grace*. Every damn time. I didn't always know or live by this belief. There was one tragic, soul-shifting and life-altering event that brought me home. It taught me that I am part of an infinite Cosmos far bigger than my human self. I was already on a journey of deep awakening, in preparation for what was to come (or accelerated because of it)?

Our daughter was baby number four in our family. She followed three little boys. She was so long-awaited and her brothers, daddy and I were beyond excited for her arrival. After all, we had known of her existence since I had first dreamed of her eight years earlier. In that dream, I was clearly shown her name *Amelia Jade*, written out in chalk on a driveway. I would then "see" her in the faces of random little girls with curly blonde hair out in the world. Often, when my head would turn involuntarily to see a little girl standing with her family, smiling and staring back at me, I'd be left with this notion that the Universe was handing me a signal.

We knew she was coming. It was just a matter of *when*. Finally, after eight years of waiting, I told my husband she was ready to come. He knew by now to trust me. That same month we conceived her. Fast forward to July 27, 2017, one day over her due date. I was finally on the way to the hospital in *very* active labour. We were ready to meet the soul we had so long waited for. In hindsight, I should have felt excited about our dream finally coming true. The only way I can describe the feeling I had on route to the hospital, was an emptiness and a feeling of doom. Up until the last few weeks before her birth, there was so much excitement. Then suddenly, I just couldn't visualise her in the baby capsule or in her bassinet. I just couldn't imagine her in our life past her birth. There was a stillness, an eerie sense of knowing that our world was about to change.

We pulled up and rushed into the Pregnancy Assessment Unit. As we were led into the consultation room, I was contracting with only a 10 to 30-second break in between. Leading up to the birth, I was preparing myself for a much sacred birth than I had experienced with my three sons. I had participated in a Sacred Birthing Program, so I felt very prepared for a divine and powerful birth complete with soothing music, meditation, crystals, and a powerful mindset. I told the midwife I was hoping for a water birth, and she started getting that ready with the other birth-suite staff.

She came back in with a doppler (a monitor that gets placed on the mother's belly to detect the baby's heart rate), and while I was fully focused on breathing through the intensity of the contractions, she put the machine on my bump to trace a heartbeat. I was standing and contracting powerfully, so after a few minutes of her not being able to find a heartbeat, I wasn't concerned. After a few minutes, she decided to call in the Registrar doctor with a scanner. The doctor came in. The midwife stood to my left, with the doctor to my right, with the medical scanner facing towards both of them. My husband sat on a chair next to me. All three displayed meek, poker faces.

Another few seconds of silence passed, and the Registrar said she was going to get a more senior doctor. The next doctor came in and started scanning. I was still strangely calm. I looked at the first doctor who stood at the foot of the bed and I remember so clearly how she slowly pulled out what looked like a walkie-talkie and held it close to her face. That was the moment I knew something was wrong and everything slowed to a standstill. Time, space and the very air in the room seemed to disappear. The excruciating labour pain seemed non-existent for those few seconds. I blurted out loudly, "What's going on?", and that's when the second doctor put her hand on my knee and told me, "I'm so sorry, there is no heartbeat."

This is the moment that changed my life forever. "I'm so sorry darling, she's gone," she said succinctly. "What do you mean? She's right there. Look at my belly, she's right there. Find her!" I yelled, as if they were talking about something they had lost in the forest. Now there was another doctor in the room. A man, this time. Maybe he could find her, I thought. His words to me were soft and kind, but very firm. I begged him to cut her out of me. He told me he was the most senior doctor in the maternity hospital that night, and in his 17 years of obstetrics, he had always been able to convince a mother to continue with naturally birthing her stillborn child. He proceeded to outline all the reasons why. At this point, I didn't care.

You hear stories of primal screams when a mother loses her young in the wild. I have come to learn humans are no different. Even in the confines of the most pristine manmade settings, we are in essence wild, free animals. In those first moments, I made sounds I had never heard come out of my, or any other human's, mouth. I hope I never hear them again. Those raging, primitive noises were followed by the most extraordinary experience of my life. A vibration entered my body. I now know it to be the highest vibration there is; *Universal Source Energy*, or *God*. It reverberated through every cell in my being! It still echoes in my ear when I recall it loudly saying, "Everything is actually going to be okay!" Somehow, I trusted it to be true. I felt divine energy surrounding me and I called upon my guides and angels to be there and support me. I wasn't sure how I was going to birth a baby who wasn't alive, and I knew I couldn't do it on my own in my human form. I knew I needed help from the *Light*. I went on to deliver the most divine baby girl. She was blonde with gorgeous lips and round cheeks. I birthed the most beautiful angel. She was grace, beauty and magic all rolled into one. Everything about her was perfect. Everything, except for the stillness.

I can recall every second of every minute of every hour that followed for the next 24 hours. We got to spend the next few hours holding her, crying together and adoring every inch of her small body. My husband bathed her with the midwife, and the midwife dressed her in the first of two outfits she would ever wear. Holding my baby girl, I stared in wonder at her perfection. I wept and wondered why? I questioned everything, including what I could have done to have caused this. It was such a surreal feeling both wanting to hold this baby forever, but at the same time wanting to be so far away.

I remember the smell in the birth-suite and our hospital room. I remember the suppleness of her skin. I remember thinking how much softer it was than my baby boys' skin. I remember how any warmth in her soon turned cold. I remember watching her beautiful plump lips turn hard and dark. I remember how long her fingers were. I remember being torn between wanting to hold her forever, and not wanting to hold her at all. I kept picking her up then putting her fragile body back in the cold cot (a special Moses-type bassinet with a cooling system to preserve a stillborn baby's body). I remember knowing she would come back. The piece of information I received from that voice, confirmed that as truth to me.

Around 2:00 am of the next morning following Amelia's birth, was a moment that shifted my perspective forever. As the book *A Course in Miracles*[1] refers to it, it was *a miracle*. I was shown a distinct vision of the future, accompanied by a knowing and an understanding of why. I was sitting wide awake with glazed eyes, feeling exhausted having had no sleep for 48 hours straight. I looked online to see if there was anyone to talk to. Strangely the only one on Facebook Messenger was a woman I hadn't spoken to in years. I remembered that she had lost a baby herself. I sent her a message, and it was during this conversation that I had the confirmation that our Amelia would return to us. Return in another body, not the same one of course, not a replacement daughter, but the same essence or soul that had been with us for such a short time. I didn't know why Amelia couldn't have simply stayed with us, but I knew there was a reason far bigger than I could comprehend. So, this is what I held onto.

---

[1] *A Course in Miracles*, Combined Volume, Third Edition as published by the Foundation for Inner Peace.
Editor Helen Schucman, Bill Thetford, Kenneth Wapnick
Author There is no author attributed to *ACIM*, although it was "scribed" by Helen Schucman
Publisher 1976 (New York: Viking: The Foundation for Inner Peace) 2007 (The Foundation for Inner Peace, 3rd ed.)

During the days, months and years following Amelia's birth and death, each of us in our family (myself, my husband and our boys), have all had to deal with things that are just not natural. The autopsy of Amelia's little body and the awful decision to allow her brain to be removed along with planning a funeral and writing a eulogy for your own child and sister. All of this is not the *normal* process of things. Saying goodbye to her body forever and watching your other children deal with the death of a sibling, in a way they shouldn't have to, is just simply beyond difficult. However, it has also been empowering to witness how strong it has made each of my children. I have since learned how to live with my heart expanded between heaven and earth. Grief is a funny thing. You don't know how you will deal with it until you are facing it head-on. Finding *Grace* in grief is an extraordinary thing; a task set for extraordinary people.

What I want others facing a loss of this magnitude to know is, it's possible to not only survive following an event like this, but to thrive! This journey has shown me power, strength and magic beyond what I thought I was capable of. It has also changed my perception of life. I can see the beauty that surrounds us in every single moment, and every day I choose to show up. Show up for the lows to feel them and to move through them. Please don't quash those intense and raw emotions. For once you move through those lows, you will feel those magical highs.

There is a saying I heard as a child: *Those who have suffered are able to see the stars shine that much brighter in the night.* Every moment of my life since has been a reaction to the catalytic event that altered my life. I vow to live a life of *Grace*, reverence and beauty in honour of my daughter. Further, to teach and be an exemplar who shows others there is magic in absolutely everything. Even and especially, in the tragic.

My trauma and grief recovery didn't include a single antidepressant drug (even though I have unashamedly used them in the past), nor a single appointment with a psychologist (despite having benefited from therapy previously in my life). I did the work on the inside and found what I needed *within me*. I'm not saying my way is the way for others but for me, I knew that no counsellor or trauma expert could have met me in the depths I'd been to. So, whilst I advocate others find a therapist if they need extra support ... I just knew through this grief, I had to do all the work myself! I now use, and continue to use, my *Cosmic Connection* to Amelia and the *Infinite Greatness* (my non-local intuition), to guide every micro and macro decision I make. I now use my own torch to light my way through the darkness. In this darkness, I had a deep faith there would be *Light*. Six short months after Amelia was born, I fell pregnant again. I knew her soul would return. I kept being shown a vision of standing on stage in a packed arena with my grown daughter, inspiring and impacting thousands.

It was the hardest nine months of my life. I had severe anxiety and rushed to the hospital every time I didn't feel her move. The only way I survived was by *allowing it all*, throwing myself into full surrender to the *Divine*, and by trusting in that *Bigness* I mentioned before. I spent my days outside grounded on Mother Earth and staring up to Father Sky, praying to God to bring her home safely. I leaned deeper and deeper into my intuition knowing that, "Everything is actually going to be okay!"

It has been a fiercely wild and intense journey. I have since fine-tuned my potent connection, learning about the complex Quantum Sciences and Immutable Laws that govern our Universe. I have discovered powerful tools to shift through deep anxiety and fear and learned how to use my innate wisdom to flow through all aspects of my life. I have trained as a priestess of non-local consciousness (which means cultivating the connection between this earthly realm and the *Universal Consciousness*). I have called in various teachers, mentors and guides along the way, and found myself as my own *True North*, which is the only compass I need to find my way anyway.

There are many complex modalities and practices I know and have used. However, these I share here, are simple and the effects are profound and potent:

GROUNDING

Simply stand barefoot on the ground, dirt or grass. Hold your arms down by your sides or up in the air. Imagine a beam of light travelling down from the sky, down through the crown of your head and all the way through your body. Imagine this light continuing down through your feet and right down to the core of the earth and straight back up again. Simply take a few breaths and feel the energy of Father Sky and Mother Earth ground you.

HEART COHERENCE

Closing your eyes, take a deep breath in through your nose. Count to four and release out through your mouth counting to four again on the exhale. Repeat this breath again, this time letting out a sigh on the exhale. Repeat again with a deeper sigh on the exhale. Recall a memory, situation or event over the last 24 hours that invokes strong feelings of calm, joy, peace or bliss. It could be the laugh of a small child, the smell of your morning coffee or the way the sun feels on your forehead. It doesn't matter what it is that brings joy, just hold the feeling that moment or thought gives to you for one minute. Focus fully on it. Whenever your mind starts to wander, just bring it back to that joyful thought. Let it simmer and percolate. Take another deep breath in through the nose and out through the mouth. Open your eyes when you feel ready. You should feel more centred and your heart should be in a coherent rhythm.

JOURNALING AND CONNECTING WITH YOUR INTUITION

Following a sequence of heart coherence and sitting somewhere comfortable, take out a journal and prompt yourself with a question you need to ask yourself. This could be anything. Something as simple as, *What do I need to know right now?* Then simply allow your hand to start writing. You'll be surprised at the innate wisdom that starts pouring out.

The mission I am here for is to show it's possible to find magic in the tragic, to find grace in grief, and to shift the paradigm around loss. I am constantly told how strong I am and how gracefully I am dealing with my grief. The truth is, I believe the Universe doesn't give us these experiences to punish or destroy us. Rather, it shows what we are capable of in service of our growth. Our *Light* is our ability to love unconditionally, no matter how broken our heart is. To forgive, for when we know this power, we know the blessing of what it's truly like to be alive. I will never ever take that for granted. Life is a miracle. And I am so grateful to my daughter for showing me that.

Your Gift

Georgia Hansen provides a multi-layered approach for women to find and use their voices. As an Editor and PR/Marketing and communications expert, she shines a light on women with extraordinary stories, important messages and a mission to share.

For any woman who knows she has a story or message to share, and wants to learn more about how to write their story for media, Georgia is offering a free How To Write Your Story - Feature Writing Workbook.

georgiamhansen.com

facebook.com/georgiamhansen

instagram.com/georgia.m.hansen

Here's to strong women.
May we know them.
May we be them.
May we raise them.

~Unknown

LOUISE O'REILLY

The oppressive status quo is something Louise refuses to swallow. This Mumma-bear won't stop until she's changed the world for her babies. With her unique self-expression, heart-centred rebelliousness, and clarity of her vision of the inclusive world we could be enjoying. It's no wonder Louise is an inclusion and diversity coach, mentor and course creator for heart-centred & socially-conscious entrepreneurs.

Louise is a Warrwa-Noongar Aboriginal woman who focuses on cultural inclusion, diversity and anti-racism work for entrepreneurs—offering the Inclusion Creators Collective membership. It's filled with courses, live trainings, group coaching and more. Louise also offers limited 1:1 coaching services. Her dream is the co-creation of a more inclusive world through social innovation. Where everyone feels free and safe to be themselves. Her drive is her children, her cheer-squad is her husband and her inspiration is her inner-calling. Louise's coaching is gentle, inclusive, and compassionate. LouiseOReilly.com.au is where you'll find her blogs, free trainings, videos, podcasts, and services.

Outside of business, Louise was freelance writing for Amnesty International Australia, radio hosting on Noongar Radio, a Miss NAIDOC Perth finalist, and is currently part of an Australian-first, Aboriginal-led visionary 10-year project creating social change and reconciliation in Boorloo (Perth).

INCLUSIVE RIPPLES AND CHANGING THE WORLD

I didn't belong and I was powerless to change it. There was something about me that just didn't fit in. On a daily basis, I was pushed away, excluded and unwelcome because of my race. My racial identity as an Aboriginal woman is integral to the makeup of my essence. It's also the place of much confusion and pain. I have white skin and I am Aboriginal. The love-hate relationship with my identity has transformed into a powerful purpose of inspiring acceptance and inclusion in the world. I am now able to stare racism in the eye and say, "I'm not afraid anymore!" after previously feeling powerless. I used to be convinced that one person could not change culture, societal norms or the world. I believed that the racially-fuelled mistreatment of others was something that couldn't be transformed. I was emotionally beaten into submission to accept racism as part of everyday life.

As a little girl, I remember standing in my year one classroom. It was after school, the class was empty, and I stood there looking up at Mum speaking to my teacher. We had been learning about Captain Cook and the first colonial settlement in Australia. My mum asked why we weren't also being taught history from an Aboriginal perspective. Simply put, my teacher said she was not allowed to because it wasn't in the curriculum. Confusion filled my little head and I kept asking the question *why?* in my mind.

At six years old, I was pushed to accept a strange concept of self-identity much earlier than a child should be. An adult asked me if I was Aboriginal or non-Aboriginal, I said, "Both!" The response back started an unnecessary inner-turmoil about my sense of belonging in both cultures: "You're Aboriginal or you're not, you can't be both!" they said. I couldn't understand how one heritage line could erase another. I felt like part of me was stripped away because I had to choose one. This person's idea of identity was based on outdated "dinosaur-thinking"; of governmental policies like the White Australia policy of 1901, the Assimilation policy of 1961 and the Aborigines Act of 1844 that enforced cultural genocide, coerced assimilation and forced child removal ideologies.

Growing up, I observed daily casual racism in general conversation. It painted Aboriginal people as lazy; dumb; trouble-makers; substance-abusers; and dole-bludgers. And yes, these are the exact terms used. Offensive words like *Abo, boong, coon, half-caste* and similar, were everyday language. Other times, these words weren't said to me directly. Instead, I would read between the lines because they would speak to me in a particular demeaning tone. Mostly, it came across as microaggressions, like the presumption that an Aboriginal woman would have children but not a job. Or, that if an Aboriginal person had a nice house or car, that it was given to them by the government (oh, how misinformed and ridiculous that one is!).

What hurt most of all, was listening to blatant racism from the people I loved. My whole life I was exposed to their hateful words and thoughts as they complained about Aboriginal people. They insulted the Aboriginal community and would make racist jokes, which meant they were about me too. Worst of all, they would joke about killing and murdering Aboriginal people. They would follow up by saying, "...but not you! You're one of the *good ones*." Well, I'm not the exception to the Aboriginal community and the truth is, their love for me does not excuse their racist words, actions and behaviours. With the daily barrage of racism in every space, it's something I couldn't escape. Not even in my own home. Racism would blast out from the TV and radio, and was openly practised within my own family. Everyday social messaging that Aboriginal people are bad, wrong and unwelcome, soon had me believing it about myself. I hated myself and the blood that flowed through my veins. I felt conflicted: I didn't belong here — yet, this was my country and my home.

Through my teens, these compounding experiences hurt so much. I thought denying my Aboriginality would surely ease my pain and suffering. If I weren't what everyone hated, I would be what everyone loved, right? Perhaps I'd be accepted and finally belong. So, I pushed away my Aboriginality. I shoved it deep, deep down and hid it away. I tried to be what society wanted. I tried to be the good-girl by following all the rules and not rocking the boat. I tried to conform my way of being in the world so that I could belong. It didn't work. The rejection of my Aboriginality was soul-crushing. I was reduced to nothing but a shell of a human, I was empty on the inside. As I lay in bed at night, I prayed that I would die during my slumber so that I wouldn't have to go through the turmoil of another day feeling powerless to the self-hatred and rejection induced by society.

It was drummed into me to accept *what is,* and I did. I grew up, married the love of my life and was happy as long as I accepted racism as a part of everyday life. Little did I know, a moment in time was soon approaching, which would change everything. We became pregnant with our first of two children. It was a magical time of joy and love. I was in bliss until the moment reality hit me, and it hit me hard! I was going to birth my child into a world filled with normalised racism and hate. A place where Australian societal systems; foundations of business; language and the culture at large, were built on the oppression of Aboriginal people and other marginalised groups. I didn't want my children to go through the same pain and trauma I went through growing up. I committed to doing everything in my power to protect my children. Even if that meant I had to change the world.

We moved to Boorloo (Perth, Western Australia) when I was six months pregnant. This was when the dreams started. For over five years, I had a recurring dream of my Ancestors in ceremonial dress. They danced around a campfire in the dark of night and one would step forward presenting two objects to me. In one hand was a large oblong wooden shield with white painted dots and in the other, was a conch shell horn. I didn't know what the dream meant, but I knew it was important.

On my twenty-ninth birthday, I felt like an empty shell of nothingness again. I had made little to no progress in changing the world for my children. I felt unfulfilled. I had a business that wasn't aligned to my soul mission, and I had no idea who I was other than a mum. I had lost myself again, clutching to the promise made to my children and unveiling the meaning behind my dream. I dedicated the next year to my own self-discovery. I was a little wiser this time and knew I had to find 'me' first, before I could impact the world in the way I wanted.

A few months later, a shaman took me on a shamanic meditative journey. This experience was a pivotal moment in my story because that journey took me back to my dream. It allowed me to ask my Ancestors questions. I finally received the answers I needed. My Ancestors told me the shield represented protection and the conch represented bringing awareness. They were being bestowed on me. They were life mission gifts, and I could choose to accept or decline their offering. I chose to accept the shield and the conch, to protect my culture, share our voices and bring awareness to the plight of our lived experience in modern Australia.

Soon after, I began blogging about human rights and more specifically, Aboriginal rights. I also began sharing my experiences as a fair-skinned Aboriginal woman. Although this felt like a big step, I knew I was still holding back. I knew there was more of me to give, and I wasn't allowing my light to shine through. I felt the pull to take things to the next level. To inspire people into uplifting, meaningful action that would inclusively impact humanity. Something that was more than just sharing knowledge, information and personal experiences. It needed to be a ground-swelling social movement, where people were so deeply inspired by the vision of what we could create together that they couldn't help but join our global community of *inclusion-creators*. I knew this was my life mission and my soul purpose, but I was scared. It seemed so big, scary, and frankly unrealistic.

In 2020, my world was thrown upside down and my heart was torn to shreds. I experienced massive personal losses that stripped so many layers off me, I could no longer hide from myself. I put my whole life, my choices and all my relationships under a microscope. It was the "great crumbling" of myself. I realised who I had created wasn't a true reflection of my authentic self. Rather, I had built a version of who I thought I should be, based on the expectations of others and society. I 'injected' myself with an imaginary *good-girl-toxin* that coerced me to follow society's rules, to not speak up, to smile and pretend everything was okay. This version of me was designed to please others, to change myself in ways to satisfy what they wanted. My logic was that they might accept me and then maybe I would belong. As it turns out, I was wrong! And that's okay.

At the time my heart was breaking, but I knew that "crumbling" had to happen. I knew I had to allow the old me to be torn away and that I had to help tear her down. The old version wasn't the best version of me. It wasn't the version I wanted to be for my children or my husband. It wasn't a version that could fulfil my life purpose. I needed to create an authentic version of myself that aligned with my soul. It needed to be a version that loved and accepted me unconditionally. One that would support me in achieving my dreams, goals, potential and in fulfilling my soul mission.

I started building myself from the foundation up. I dived internally into the core values, belief systems and ideologies that made up my identity. I uncovered there, stories that kept me playing small and feeling unworthy. I found social conditioning that told me I wasn't enough and that some people were better than others. I found unconscious biases that told me to be fearful of different groups of people. This is why I searched for outside validation of my worthiness and belonging. I could see with clarity that none of this was mine. It was all just beliefs and limitations from others that contributed to the prevention of me becoming the 'me' I was born to be. Bit by bit, I released what did not serve me.

It was liberating and exhilarating to detach from the egoistic version of myself. I allowed the expectation, social constructs and inauthenticity to fall away from me. I had let go of all the things that I allowed to hold me back. I released the fear of being judged, being rejected and failing. The real me started to shine through, and I began to realise my unlimited power. I could choose whatever I desired of myself. I could choose happiness; joy; fulfilment; unconditional love and acceptance. I could choose to know and own my belonging.

I made the decision to transform my blogging into something that would motivate the minds and souls of business owners. I wanted to create a platform that would inspire inclusive-action that was change-making, soul-aligning and positively-meaningful for Aboriginal people and other marginalised groups. By releasing what no longer served me, I was able to speak about important things like racism, inclusion, equity and diversity with a clarity and a confidence I had not yet experienced. I could speak about these issues, in all their complexities, in a simple way. Now when I speak, I am 100% guided by my intuition. I come alive and am in a complete flow state. I feel connected to the universe and feel its energy surging through me. My soul is joyous when I teach, coach and mentor others about racism, inclusion, equity and diversity. It is my calling, and I surrender wholeheartedly to it.

Interestingly, I had previously been involved in activism and protests, yet it never felt right for me. These events were filled with injustice; anger; rage; pain and suffering. They were organised in ways to place blame. I felt these movements turned up the levels of sadness, guilt and shame, while being riddled with empathic inaction and powerlessness. Not only does this type of change-making not align with who I am, but it contradicts the Law of Attraction. Based on that Law, the low-frequencies these actions emit can only attract more of that type of energy into the world. My business is based on acknowledging the past, learning from it and looking to the future. It focuses on asking what type of world we want to be creating through our businesses. It's based on love; compassion; freedom; liberation; acceptance and inclusion. It's a high-vibrational way of creating change. It is all about social impact and social innovation in a way I've never seen done before. It starts from a place within, to uncover my client's values; beliefs; unconscious biases; social conditionings and most importantly, their privilege. For me, the most terrifying thing is people who don't understand the power and impact their privilege has on the lives of marginalised people. This is where I help entrepreneurs understand their privilege and harness it in their business to create powerful and positive change in a way that's meaningful, impactful and fulfilling to them. The truth is social change doesn't have to be loud, bold or confronting. It doesn't have to feel heavy and be laced with guilt, shame or anger. It can be gentle, warm and inviting. And, it most certainly can be embedded with love, acceptance, freedom and happiness.

The secret about changing the world is everyone can do it. You change the world when you choose to think, do or behave in a soul-aligning way. When you choose to adjust your language to be inclusive of marginalised groups, you're changing the world. When you choose to add captions to your videos or install disability access, you're increasing accessibility and changing the world. When you choose to share an Acknowledgment of Country, you're showing respect to the Aboriginal and Torres Strait Islander communities and in turn, changing the world. When you offer different payment options, you are removing barriers that exclude people with less money. It's these decisions to be inclusive, and take inclusive action, that ultimately changes the world.

The amazing thing is your actions ripple out into the world and inspire others to be more inclusive too. Your vision of an inclusive world becomes their vision too. They take that love and acceptance into their homes, their workplaces and their communities where they ripple it out even further. This is a positive social movement that's not dependent on governments or policies. It's one that is birthed from the people.

A beautiful ripple was shared with me after I gave an online presentation. I spoke about the possibilities of making business more inclusive. This led one participant to start a discussion about business inclusivity with their own family around the dinner table. By opening this conversation, their teen shared that they identified as non-binary. Prior, the teen had been afraid to say anything, as they didn't know if the family would understand or accept them. The family was loving and accepting. That teen felt so supported that they shared their non-binary identity with their peers. This conversation led to two more teens opening up about their identity and their fears about telling others, including their parents. Those teens were loved, accepted and supported, which allowed them to feel more confident in freely expressing themselves. It has brought so much love, community and connection into their worlds. It blows my mind to think how many people's lives were positively impacted by a single conversation, and by a single action. Imagine the positive ripples that your actions could make?

Through my childhood traumas; becoming a mother; dreaming a dream; my own "great crumbling" and the soul-aligned recreation of me, I now know my place in this world. I know my purpose, and how I can positively inspire social change. I have clarity around my vision and what I want to evoke in the world. I know with every fibre of my being that I am powerful and that I belong. I have the power to change the culture of our society because I have seen the inclusive world we will create. The reason its creation is inevitable is because of business owners like you, who share that same vision. A world where everyone is free to be themselves authentically without fear of discrimination. A world where our similarities and differences are celebrated. Where everyone is accepted, valued and included. A world where everyone belongs. Every single person has the power to change the world. Are you going to change the world today?

Your Gift

If you're a business owner and your soul said "YES" Louise would love to support you in evoking the clarity and confidence required for your inclusive world-changing business actions. She is gifting you one month free access into the Inclusion Creators Collective membership. There you'll find training videos and downloadable resources. During the month you'll also get a LIVE group coaching session, a week of guided inclusive business actions and a LIVE group development session, all while being warmly welcomed into her online member community space. Use the code 'ripple' through the following link to gain access louise-oreilly.thinkific.com/courses/membership

Connect with Louise at: www.LouiseOReilly.com.au

JO BANGLES

Today I can sit comfortably in the skin of an empowered woman but growing up; I didn't have any idea about the kind of power I held. Becoming an adult and claiming my identity showed me that my power comes from many places. Now that I am older, I can see that it started with my mother and grandmother. I now recognise the strength and tenacity they wielded effortlessly, and it's no wonder that I am unwavering in my convictions. Coming out in the face of discrimination and prejudice during my early adulthood led me to a community that taught me the courage and power to live my truth. I have always had the luxury of being surrounded by empowered people.

As I continue to learn and grow, I feel stronger, more balanced and more confident every day, knowing that I am capable of tremendous things. As a leader and a strong woman — I relish the opportunity to role model the kind of confidence and empowerment that I now see as having fuelled me my whole life. Empowered women empower other women, and I am proud to be part of that ongoing exchange.

Even though there are many fights left to tackle in the journey to equality as a lesbian and as a woman, claiming my power allows me to experience the freedom to live my life authentically and for myself.

Jo Bangles, Queerpreneur, is one of the most recognisable faces in the Australian LGBTQIA+ community and a thriving entrepreneur. Growing up in a tough neighbourhood, Jo learned early on to stand up for herself. She has travelled the world in the name of diversity and inclusion and is on a journey to pass on her leadership story to the next generation.

thejobanglesproject.com

LISA FOGGON

Lisa Foggon is an empowered woman, mother to two beautiful young boys with another on the way, a registered nurse and midwife and a successful online business mentor. She devotes a large amount of her time to helping women see their power and potential when it comes to making an impact on their own lives and the world. In both roles as a midwife and online business mentor Lisa guides women on their own journey to empowerment and knowing their worth. Lisa takes great honour in helping women find their voice and realising they have choice, more freedom and opportunity within their grasp.

Empowered Women Empower

I was put on this earth to empower you to realise your strength, girlfriend! Life events, including brain surgery to treat debilitating epilepsy and the rollercoaster journey to motherhood, has helped me come to this conviction.

I knew I wanted to make a career out of helping people from a young age. That's one of the reasons why I chose to become a nurse after leaving school. Later I became a midwife, and more recently an online business mentor. Though as I look back on my high school years, I do recall believing that all I was destined for was something very standard. My self-esteem wasn't great, and I saw myself as an average student who wasn't going to achieve much more than a typical career path. You see, at the time a small reason I chose a nursing career was because I saw it as an easy career option that held minimal risk of failing.

Even though I had to complete university, I thought it was one of the easiest ways to gain a bachelor's degree and get that graduation cap on my head. I would be one of the few in our large extended family to attend university and I saw this to most likely be the height of my success. I now know that I was very wrong in thinking my degree would be my sole greatest achievement, and that I would live an average life. Life was about to teach me a few lessons and show me the incredible strength I was yet to recognise deep inside.

At around the age of 18, I was living away from home in a small country town in New South Wales, Australia. There, I was undertaking my nursing training when I was diagnosed with a rare form of epilepsy. My seizures involved me frequently losing my awareness, becoming blank and not responding. Sometimes I would lose control of my bladder and wet myself (usually at the most inconvenient and embarrassing of places). I experienced repetitive movements of my hands and mouth, rapid onset of exhaustion (I would always have to sleep it off for a few hours afterwards). The episodes always resulted in debilitating and worsening memory loss. Suddenly, I'd lost my valued independence. It was deemed unsafe for me to drive a car and I was failing my nursing degree. It was no longer safe for me to carry out daily tasks alone. I felt like such a burden to my family and friends.

Over a period of about five years I had trialled every medication there was, and in numerous combinations, whilst enduring debilitating side effects including chronic fatigue and weight gain followed by rapid weight loss. I quickly learnt to treasure photos as these were (and still are) a great tool to ignite what little memories I had, and still have of such events. This included my twenty-first birthday as well as travels locally and abroad.

By the time I had turned twenty-four, the seizures were progressively getting worse. Some days seizures would occur up to three times a day. All treatment options had been exhausted over the 3-4 years prior with my original neurologist. After patiently sitting a twelve-month waitlist, I was finally able to see a different neurologist for a second opinion. What he had in mind was not at all what I had expected. The appointment was short, with the doctor promptly suggesting I could be a suitable candidate for brain surgery to treat my epilepsy. Further that, he would like to refer me to a neurosurgeon and epilepsy treatment team in Sydney.

Brain surgery! Who knew that was a treatment for epilepsy? I remember my initial thought was something like, "No way!" But at that point, I had no other options apart from carrying on the way I had been, and that certainly wasn't sustainable. So, I said yes to the referral and within a few months I found myself nervously sitting in front of the Associate Professor of Neurological Surgery in Sydney, alongside my ever-supportive mum and dad.

The surgeon had a lovely manner. He was kind but confident. I remember it not taking long to feel safe in his care, even in the beginning. He explained that prior to the surgery, I would need to undergo a series of tests to decide whether this was a viable operation for me to undergo. As there were numerous criteria to meet, testing would take months to complete. Knowing it would be a slow step-by-step process, and that it would not be a decision for me to make if I didn't fit the criteria, strangely gave me a feeling of ease. At that point, I had nothing to lose by undergoing the testing process.

When the first round of testing commenced, I was to spend at least one week in hospital in the epilepsy unit. I would be in a bed with padded high sides, surrounded by cameras aimed at me and electrodes stuck all over my head. The electrodes created a constant Electroencephalogram (EEG) trace which picked up any seizure activity and plotted them on a graph. During this time, the aim was for my seizures to be monitored by the medical staff, so that the EEG could pinpoint where in my brain the seizures were originating from. Over the years there was one consistent trigger that contributed to my seizures... tiredness. So, throughout that week I was to have minimal sleep to create an optimal condition for inducing a seizure. During the entire week, I was to stay in bed and my mum who was assigned with the important task of pressing a handheld button if I had a seizure. The moment she pressed the button, the lights turned on, the cameras filmed, the EEG recorded, and nurses rushed in to inject a radioactive isotope into my veins.

We ended up having to do this entire week's routine twice, as it was proving difficult for the doctors and their team to pinpoint exactly where in my brain my seizures were originating. They were able to isolate that my right temporal lobe (the lower back of my brain, towards my right ear) was the concern. However, they could not pinpoint precisely the exact origin within that region. They concluded that further testing was required.

The next step was to undergo a procedure that was used as a last resort. The team proposed I go in for one more round of testing. However, this time they would surgically place the EEG electrodes on the surface of my brain, under my skull where there would be much less interference. I would remain in bed for a few days with my head bandaged dramatically, until they were confident they had located the precise origin of my seizures. The plan would then be to surgically remove the section of my brain that was causing the seizures at the same time they removed the electrodes.

Woah! Sh*t just got serious. You see, the section of my brain that they proposed to be removed was right next to my visual field. Yep! Apart from the obvious complications that come along with brain surgery, there was a significant risk that I could lose part of my vision. At the very worst, it could leave me blind. This wasn't a decision I could make in the time between the surgeries. If I was going to undergo the initial surgery, it made sense that I should also undergo the epilepsy treating surgery (if deemed possible by the medical team). Mum drove us home, back to the country, where I was to make the biggest decision of my life that far.

I found myself a quiet, safe place to think. Here, I was only twenty-four years young, contemplating what it was that I wanted out of life. I recall my thought processes bringing it down to the very basics. I asked myself what was most important to me in life? What was it that I wanted to achieve? And what option was going to allow me to achieve that?

I quickly concluded that family was in fact the most important thing to me. I wanted to be a loving and nurturing mother one day, and if I were having numerous seizures, I would not be able to provide a safe environment for my children. I had a fearful vision of me as a mother having a seizure whilst baking where one of my future children got burned from the oven, as I was not capable of supervising appropriately. I also had concerns around how the medications I had been prescribed, could affect a future pregnancy.

I had fleeting doubts of whether I was worthy of all this fuss and pressure I was placing on my loved ones. That was quickly shut down by my parents. Going ahead with the brain surgery I had originally scoffed at, now seemed like a risk I was willing to take for the sake of my own, and my future family. With the possibility of losing half of my vision (or worse) during surgery, I believed I would still be able to care for my future children safely as I had envisioned, even if it were with support. So with that, we booked the surgeries. Kliff (my boyfriend at the time) and I travelled to Europe for a pre-surgery, fun-filled adventure before we came home to attempt a better life for us all.

Prior to the London Olympics in 2012, I underwent the first round of surgery. The electrodes did what the team had hoped. They were able to pinpoint exactly which part of my brain needed to be removed. It was still possible I could lose half, or all, of my vision. However, this time the surgeon instilled great confidence in me, as he had done the first time we met. He reassured me that things would be okay. My instincts told me the same. I put all my trust into the surgeon and his team. This is something I still struggle with to this day, as I very much like to be in control. Whether I knew it or not at the time, I was undergoing a personal transformation. And, from this point on, there was no going back to that young woman who thought herself worthy of only average achievements.

I don't recall much from that week, but I do remember the looks on my family's faces when I was being wheeled into surgery to remove that troublesome, golf-ball-sized section of my brain. I made a conscious effort to use my pre-surgery vision to impress the faces of the people I cared for most onto my memory, in case I was to lose my sight and never see them again. I can still envision them looking scared, but somehow brave, whilst radiating support and pride. I've since seen a glimpse of a similar look on my father's face when he walked me down the aisle to marry Kliff.

The surgery took several hours but for me, it felt like seconds. I recall opening my eyes and being overwhelmed with sheer relief. My vision appeared to be perfect! I cried some of the happiest tears in my life in that recovery room. As soon as I saw my family and with tears of gratitude trickling down my face, I announced loudly, "I can see normally!"

It turned out my visual field was impaired slightly with a loss to my left upper quadrant of sight. These days on the exceedingly rare occasion, I might bump the left side of my head on a high shelf or kitchen cabinet. An after-effect I can live with! I had one seizure in the week following the surgery, but doctors reassured me this was okay. I am proud to say that I have not had a seizure since.

Within the year following the surgery, I was granted my driver's licence back. I graduated my Bachelor of Nursing degree; had gained a sought-after post-graduate position in a large Sydney hospital; and I'd scored myself an engagement ring. I even made the bold choice to wean myself off the medication the doctors suggested I stay on for at least five more years. "Pfff, yeah right!" I thought to my newly empowered self. I had a strong belief they didn't work anyway. I had not only gained my valued independence back, but also a whole new lease on life. From then on, nothing was going to hold me back!

I am exceptionally grateful I was brave enough to say yes to the surgery. I would not lead the incredible life I do today without taking that risk. I would not be the mother, support or inspiration I am today without having gone through these difficulties. Some may see my journey as unfortunate. I see the opposite. If I had not been granted this journey, I would still think of myself as that average and unworthy young lady I once did. That would be a tragedy, not only for myself but every person that I have since had contact with, including the generations of my family that will follow.

I felt on top of the world and incredibly empowered. The surgery was like a portal to me, allowing me to realise that I could do anything and succeed in this world. I trusted my instincts and brought the decision-making process right down to the very basics. I likened it to that scene in *The Notebook* where Noah is shouting to Ally, "What do you want?" She replies, "It's not that simple!" But as the movie continues Ally learns that it can in fact, *be that simple*. And, she too releases all judgement and expectations of others and uncovers what she really wants from her life.

I soon recognised the immense value of feeling empowered at this elevated level. It makes you realise your worth and strength. It is something I wish every person to experience during their lifetime. I now possess a knowing that I will succeed at anything I set my mind to, if I don't run away when it becomes scary, seems impossible or even risky. This knowing was strongly reinforced after birthing our beautiful babies — but more on that another time.

The level of empowerment I am talking about here does not come easily. As you've read in my story, feeling this exuberant does not present itself without overcoming feelings of unworthiness, judgement, fear or risk. Unfortunately, it is easy for women to lose faith in their capabilities and trust in their bodies. It's no wonder we are conditioned to be ashamed of our extraordinary bodily functions, are tormented by our body image and are not educated around the importance of harnessing and honouring our monthly cycles. This is why I chose to navigate my career towards midwifery. And in more recent times, mentoring in the online business space. In both roles I educate, support and empower women to find their strength; to push past any fears or blocks that may be holding them back during some of the most daunting, difficult, yet revolutionary times in their lives.

We can do extraordinary things when we are supported, knowledgeable and shown a proven method to reaching our worthy desires, no matter how difficult the journey. This is what I can provide for all women, a pathway to reaching their greatest dreams whether that be an empowered journey into motherhood or an empowered journey to financial and time-freedom. This allows them to be the present mother they've always envisioned or to simply live a life of their own design. Due to my journey of empowerment, I was able to find the bravery to do just that. I designed a life for myself and our family, abundant with financial- and time-freedom. I released all judgement and leapt into an online business. Now I can choose to support women in a midwifery role out of passion and not simply for financial gain.

These days we choose to use our time-freedom to travel and experience our beautiful country from our comfortable family caravan, whilst still earning a healthy income along the way. When it comes down to life or death (or in my case brain surgery), we think about what means most to us. I'm sure most people don't want to reach the end of their lives before they realise that they haven't achieved what they truly desire because they weren't brave or empowered enough to try something new or scary.

Your Gift

Whatever those dreams may be - Lisa works with individuals to leverage the online space to realise their worth and guide them on a journey to empowerment. Lisa teaches others a proven method of running a successful, high-profit online business (monthly five-figure) via the use of affiliate marketing and social media. She guides women to harness the strength of their own unique, personal brand from anywhere in the world. She believes that each of you already encompasses the power needed to share your offerings with the world. Please contact Lisa if you are interested in accessing options that will assist you in reaching your greatest desires, in less time than you think.

www.instagram.com/a_mumma_empowered

ERIKA CRAMER

Being an empowered woman means that you are aware of your power. That you believe in your ability to use your power. That you are deserving of power. An empowered woman has a deep sense of self-belief and confidence in who she truly is. She fights for what she believes, and she stands for her values.

Empowered women are trailblazers and change-makers, and just by existing, they empower other women to rise. The motto of an empowered woman is "if you want to empower others, you first must empower yourself".

For so many of us, we have felt disempowered most of our lives, believing the negative thoughts that we're not enough or that we're too much. When you've done the internal work to shift these thoughts and question the "I am not good enough" narrative, that's when you start changing your reality. That's when your world shifts, and that's when you become the example of what's possible for other women.

Empowered women take responsibility for their lives, their happiness and their results. Empowered women raise confident and empowered children. Empowered women rise and help other women rise. Every woman has the ability to step away from the disempowerment and into the birthright that is our joy, freedom and empowerment.

Known as the Cardi B of the personal development world, Erika Cramer aka The Queen of Confidence is a full-flavoured, spicy inspirational speaker and mentor to thousands of women across the globe. Today, she connects with an engaged global community and shares with tens of thousands of women daily to help empower, encourage and inspire them to step into their confidence.

But it hasn't always been this way. Having survived many traumatic experiences in her youth, Erika spent many years searching for love, peace and validation in all the wrong places. She has survived childhood sexual abuse, being brought up in and out of the foster care system, life-altering car accidents, and much grief and loss.

In the last decade or so, she has been able to turn her life around from one of hopelessness and pain to one of passion, growth and success, after going on her own powerful journey of personal healing.

An international confidence coach, Erika also hosts a five-star-rated podcast, The Confidence Chronicles, which is in the top 10 of the Australian Apple charts for Mental Health, with 1,000,000+ downloads and counting, and listeners in 70+ countries.

She has created a seven-figure global business by mentoring and helping those who have suffered similar life experiences as her own.

Erika's story is one of triumph over adversity, and she is full of light, laughter and of course, confidence. Erika is a beaming and beautiful example of how you can heal your personal story to transform trauma into triumph.

Connect with Erica www.thequeenofconfidence.com

VANESA GONZALEZ-QUINONES

Vanesa Gonzalez-Quinones left her entire known world (Spain) behind to start a new life from scratch in Australia 15 years ago. While working as a soil scientist, she fell in love and started a family. However, just a few years later, her world collapsed. She found herself alone, broke and with two small kids. From her darkest time came the biggest learning: live a life that you are passionate about. She quit research, founded several companies and brought her childhood passion, the sport of Padel, to Western Australia.

FOR THE LOVE OF PADEL

It was at *Club Internacional de Tenis*, in Majadahonda, Madrid. It was 1991, where I fell in love with the sport of Padel. After moving from the island of Las Palmas (Canary Islands), where my twin sister Silvia and I were born, my parents bought a house just so we could all be close to the tennis club. As teenagers, we spent hours training and hanging out with friends at the club and competing during weekends. Playing tennis showed me so many things about determination and never giving up. Each match was a life lesson. I remember my sister winning a few tournaments. Jealous of the attention she got, I adopted the attitude of the Spanish tennis star, Arantxa Sanchez Vicario, who was known for her "vamos" and continuous positive self-encouragement. After each ball, I would encourage myself, regardless of the outcome, and what happened was magic. I started to win matches and I qualified to play at the national level. Despite the hard training and long hours, it was great fun and it forged friendships that have lasted to this day.

While hanging out after training, we would sometimes play a new sport called Padel. Padel is a racquet sport, best described as a cross between tennis and squash. It originated in Mexico in the 70s but was still relatively new in Spain at the time. By 2020, the sport had grown to be played in over 60 countries with more than 10 million regular players. But that is jumping ahead. Back in the early 90s, it was starting to explode in popularity in Spain. Padel is played in fours, making it a perfect fit for a group of teenagers who were keen on socialising. The club was for us a safe space. A place where we were welcomed; we had friends, our coach and we were part of a team. Silvia and I turned out to be quite competitive and ended up switching from tennis to Padel. For six-years running, we were national junior champions and were selected to represent Spain at the junior world championships in Buenos Aires. It was an amazing experience and a precious time in my life.

Both my parents had been married before, and I had a brother from my mum and a sister from my dad. My birth certificate showed "father unknown" because, during the dictatorship of Franco, divorce was illegal, and it was not until I was five that my parents could marry.

We lived opposite the black volcanic beaches of the Atlantic Ocean. We had freedom to roam as little kids. Signs of my brother's unhappiness became apparent around this time. He would regularly hide under our bed and scare us awake after we'd gone to sleep. I don't know if this was a reaction to his parent's divorce or just boyish pranks. However, at the time, I started having nightmares. To this day, almost every night, I awake screaming in terror from yet another nightmare. Later, I realised this reactivity in me stemmed from a term often used by psychologists to describe a person with extraordinary sensitives, a Highly Sensitive Person (HSP).

Coming from a family, whose entrepreneurial great-grandparents had everything stripped from them during World War One and the Spanish Civil War, there was a strong emphasis on getting a qualification and a safe, secure career. My parents pushed for us to complete University and to go overseas to learn English which my sister and I did. My sister Silvia, while a little more resistant to learning English, excelled at school. She had a passion for physiotherapy and knew from a young age that was what she wanted to do. I was less certain of a career path and ended up choosing Environmental Science, as suggested by my parents.

It was there, looking for something different, that I was offered a scholarship to undertake a PhD in soil quality. A few years later, having dug soil pits all over Spain and having spent hundreds of hours in the laboratory, I submitted my thesis documenting how various agricultural methods altered the microbiological and chemical indicators of soil health. I started looking further afield for adventure. With a PhD in hand, I started applying for positions and landed a job as a research scientist in the Soil Science department at the University of Western Australia. This was a turning point that led to love, children, divorce, depths of depression, self-enlightenment and new hope.

When I moved to Western Australia, life was different. I felt for the first time in life that I had the freedom to choose what I really liked, with no family pressures. I had no one and I needed to build my life from scratch. The work brought me out to the Wheatbelt of Western Australia with the dust, flies, the cool shade of the giant Karri trees in the southern forests, and the open Wandoo woodlands of the northern Jarrah Forest. My connection with the outdoors helped me feel more relaxed and calmed my big-city anxiety. I met Ryan, a passionate ecologist, in a lab surrounded by soils at the University. I had a feeling that we had met in a past life and I knew that we were going to be together. We fell in love, and under a starry night in the bush, Ryan asked me to have a baby with him. When we fell pregnant, we decided to go back to Spain as my visa was about to expire. Summer (our daughter) was born on a cold winter's day in Madrid, with snow blocking many roads in the city. This beautiful experience came with its own challenge as I had to go through a legal fight as the authorities did not want to approve the name of Summer.

Ryan and I went on to get married, however, our struggles started to show very early on in our relationship. What attracted me to him originally was his way of freely expressing what he was going through. It was so different from what I had lived in the past. Somehow, we triggered each other's fears and life together did not work. We loved each other but did not speak the same love language. I had my issues and Ryan had his struggles. However, they were soon compounded by the tragic death of his sister in a car accident. He struggled to cope and acted out, breaching our trust. In the midst of our relationship falling apart, Emily, our second daughter was conceived as we both wanted a sibling for Summer to grow up with. My life was starting to unravel at this point. I'd lost my passion for work, partly because of the constant insecurity of lack of secure funding, as well as the endlessly critical culture of academic research. I was starting to wonder, *Why do I do this? What is the benefit to humanity?* Something very important was missing, my *why*. I also felt my other creative needs were not fulfilled. Now my relationship had fallen apart and I was single, caring for a baby and a toddler, and soon to be broke.

Summer has been the catalyst for much change in my life. I started noticing that she would have regular accidents and her sensitivity to stimuli such as sound, noise and touch continued well beyond her baby stage. It made me think there was some underlying cause. When she started school, the teacher called me in to check if she talked at home. Apparently, she had gone years talking to only one friend at school. At home, she was perfectly fine and chatty, but would become frozen and unable to respond to anyone who prompted her. Teachers also noticed that she had difficulty in learning. One day my mother-in-law showed me an article about a kid that was experiencing the same as Summer. She could not talk at school or outside our home: Selective Mutism was the name of the behaviour. This condition is a type of anxiety and affects many children.

The more I learned about it, the more I could help her. Instead of encouraging her to talk, I had to tell her that it was okay if she didn't feel like talking. For a few years, I was obsessed, learning everything about her condition and new ways of helping her learn better. However, at the age of eight, things were still not right with multiple accidents and more neurological symptoms. Even numerous doctors said there was nothing to worry about, my intuition knew otherwise. I took her to a neurologist who, after a scan, diagnosed a brain injury that possibly happened during her long birth. The sense of guilt took me by surprise. In that moment I understood that her brain had to work twice as hard as an average child to do the same tasks. I decided to take her out of all the extra activities. I had to accept that we needed a new calmer approach and to let her work at her own pace.

She was beautifully perfect as she was, and being good at school became unimportant. Doing more research, I came across an article about the *Highly Sensitive Person* by Elaine Aaron that resonated with not only Summer's personality, but also my own. These people have nervous systems that overreact to everyday stimuli. The fight and flight mechanisms we have evolved with, are easily triggered and are expressed through emotional over-reactions or introversion.

After experiencing a body breakdown, an old tennis injury flared up. I was bedridden with agonising pain for a month. Then with Summer having more serious accidents, I was feeling like everything was racing at such speed that I could not hold the reins of my life. I started to loosen my control. Bit by bit as I felt completely overwhelmed. I was feeling dead inside. I asked the Universe what my path was, and to send me a clear sign. I called my dad and he told me something that stayed with me. "Your life is only yours to decide what to do with. It doesn't belong to anyone else but you. Stop everything, go to Matilda Bay and make time to think about it." And, that was exactly what I did. I asked myself, *What would I do if I won the lottery?* Weeks later, the answer came clear to me. After thinking about Ryan's sister dying, my uncle's recent cancer diagnosis and dark thoughts about my own struggles, I realised I was alive, and that I had already won the lottery. I decided to follow my passions: Padel, learning more and helping *Highly Sensitive People*.

I enrolled in the *New Enterprise Incentive Scheme* (NEIS program), an intensive three-week course teaching how to create a business. What I learned there transformed me forever. It was like a part of me, that I didn't know existed, had awakened. I entered into a world of wanting to learn more and more through workshops, meetings, talks and chats with other entrepreneurs. For me, starting a business was a form of creativity that refocused my energy. I felt that I was finally connecting with my self-confidence and found a passion within me that had been stripped away by the academic culture of self-criticism and self-doubt.

I started designing a business, marketing and social media plan. Sometimes it felt hard, however, I pushed forward and did one thing per day, even if it was only tiny steps. With my sister working continually as a contracting physiotherapist that was not well paid, we decided to put Padel sport on hold and start *Be Alive Physiotherapy*. Our family practice offered a holistic approach to treatment. From years of study, and practice Silvia had developed her own way of treating, by combining techniques from physiotherapy, osteopathy and myofascial release therapy. Her passion for learning made her seek other therapies that addressed emotional symptoms. This led us to develop a workshop specifically for *HSPs*. It was designed for *HSPs* to understand what the psychological term means and how *HSPs* can design a life around that.

Two years after starting *Be Alive* we resurrected our vision of bringing Padel to Perth. When people continued to ask me how the project was going, I realised that Padel was bigger than myself and my fears, and I had to make it happen. After getting approval for an inner-city Padel club, only to then get a change of government that caused the terms of the lease to make the project unprofitable, we had to keep looking for a suitable site. After pitching to Reabold Tennis Club, they put their trust in us and supported our planning proposal to the local government. After what seemed like hundreds of meetings, presentations and negotiations, we were given the okay to go ahead.

When I look back, the thing I found the hardest to accomplish was finding the right people. The concept of Padel was new, so many builders didn't want the challenge. When I did find one, they ended up quoting so much, my investors decided not to proceed. I spent weeks crying, feeling helpless. I found consolation in a business mentoring group that provided encouragement and advice. I had committed myself to making it happen regardless of what it took. I started from scratch: took on the role of the builder myself; sought quotes; worked out the technical details; and progressed towards a new business plan. My sister, my partner and other friends helped me with the design and a few months later, I reduced the costs to a point allowing the investors to re-sign to the project.

Padel Perth Reabold, the first Padel club in Western Australia, opened in February 2020. In the time since we opened, we have had more than 2000 players register and compete. More importantly, a Padel community is starting to grow. We finally created a space of belonging where anyone is welcome to come and exercise by having fun and connecting with others. We've also helped a new club get started, which should be up and running before the end of 2021. Now other tennis clubs and investors are approaching us to help them do the same.

One of my biggest life lessons that has helped me get through and overcome all my challenges came while climbing the Villarrica volcano in Pucon, Chile with my boss in 2008. What we experienced was the most physically challenging 10 hours of my life. We spent three hours of the five-hour climb in heavy crampons (steel spikes that attach to boots), scrambling over ice. I was exhausted, and felt like I couldn't keep going. Thinking I would freeze to death, I decided to stay with the group. The climb got steeper and steeper as we approached the top. I remember seeing another group ahead of us and someone slipped and fell only to be grabbed by a guide before she disappeared down the slope. It was the most dangerous thing I had ever done in my life. My only thoughts were "I'm going to die here". The fear felt so real that at one point, I froze to the spot, unable to move forward. In that moment, I was the most scared I had ever been. It was also when I realised that I had to switch my mind: from fear to support.

I decided to do the same as when I was playing tennis. I decided to encourage myself with every step forward that I took in my life saying, "Come on, one more step!" Instead of looking down below, to the scary view, I decided to focus on looking forward. I focused all my attention on getting to the summit. When I did, I felt a sense of power that even now is difficult to explain. I was so proud of myself. My advice to you is when everything looks scary just focus on the next step; take one step at a time. When life throws up real challenges, I think back to my time on the mountain and it helps me take the next step. It has not been an easy journey. It continues to be a real struggle to balance family and work demands. I went without an income for more than four years, as well as the increasing strain on personal relationships. So many times, I wondered if all the effort was worth it. It is worth it, especially in those moments when I hear how much fun people are having when playing Padel, the stories from the workshops we developed and that we've helped people. And then, there is Marloes, the most beautiful woman who is fighting off terminal cancer every day of her life. She comes to play when the tough days come and chooses to be active, to play with her friends and to laugh as much as she can. She says that the club is her happy place and thanks me for creating it. And that is when I realised that every single bit of struggle has been worth it. Her words become my mantra to keep going.

Connect with Vanesa

www.facebook.com/padelperth

hello@padelperthreabold.com.au

www.padelperthreabold.com.au/

The path from dreams to success does exist. May you have the vision to find it, the courage to get on it and the perseverance to follow it.

Kalpana Chawla ~ Astronaut

RADZY CHUGH

Radzy is a lifestyle coach and a Qoya movement teacher. Radzy has worked with women across the globe, leading them to live Joy-Fully. As a lifestyle coach Radzy offers many online programs and workshops supporting women to create a life they love. The focus is on how to celebrate oneself and bring Joy in living authentically. As a Qoya movement teacher, Radzy has facilitated retreats in India and offered Qoya at retreats in Bali and Fiji. Radzy received her Masters in Economics degree from New York University in 2013. Allowing Joy to fuel her choices, she chose to honour her Soul's path and ventured on as an Intuitive healer and Reiki practitioner. Radzy's Joy has led her to travel across the globe visiting Costa Rica, Iceland, Australia, Dubai, New Zealand Bali, and Fiji, participating and leading retreats.

Through her work Radzy encourages women to create a strong, transparent and committed relationship with themselves. Radzy's work revolves around supporting women to create a safe and sacred space within themselves so they can experience and express from their truth. Radzy is Nico about supporting women feeling more connected, alive and most importantly, free within themselves.

EMBODIED TRUTH

Freedom to experience and express all of who you are, this is the idea. This is the prayer. This is the vision. This is my hope, for you and for me.

You're not a fraud for wanting to grow and do better in life, and then finding at times you slip down the hole into past patterns. You're not a liar for saying you're ready, but not actually acting on it. You're not an imposter for dreaming of a you that you do not feel ready to yet be. You are a human being recognising that there is more to you than what is present in your life right now. You are in touch with a niggling voice that whispers to you every day and you feel ready to birth a new reality for yourself.

What makes you remarkable? Is it your quirks, your edge or your insights that make you like no one else? Most souls simply live day-to-day, month-to-month, year-to-year ... and finally, an entire life without ever pausing to explore the idea of who they are or what they truly desire. So many simply fail to go beyond what superficially meets the eye; to travel to that unknown part of the self that ignites their soul.

You are not that person. I believe you are *soul-driven*. You are brave and you desire to look, explore, understand and embrace what makes you so vivid and unrepeatable. Growing up, we are taught to act and behave a certain way and to be watchful of our actions. I have always been a big person. I mean physically curvaceous and voluptuous, taking up a whole lot of space. As a kid and later growing into a young adult, my culture and society informed my beliefs about myself. They were hardly encouraging or positive. "Big girls" can't wear skirts or shorts, society told me. "Big girls" should be mindful of their heavy arms, dress to cover. "Big girls" should always be on a diet and "big girls" should exercise. Socially accepted norms validate that "big girls" don't deserve to feel happy; "big girls" are doing life wrong. "Big girls" can't marry by choice, "big girls" are always second pickings. The list is ruthless and endless.

At school, time and time again, I was shoved into the last row for a dance or towards the back in a school play. I was never picked for a team during sports class. I've had school kids mock me as I walked down the road and I endured bullying in school. I grew up disliking my body and not having any relationship with it. In fact, I criticised myself often for the one thing that was not going right for me ... my body. Everybody told me what a sweet kid I was, then followed it up with some diet advice. They told me that I was good, but not good enough. I did not know whether to love myself or be mad at myself, the messages were so mixed. Was I a good person or a fat one? And because diets were sold as the answer to all my problems, I went on many.

Through the decades of my life, starting at the vulnerable age of 11, I have yo-yoed through multiple rollercoaster rides of losing and then gaining weight. Throughout this time, I did not know why I had the eating patterns I did. What caused me to eat or binge eat. I felt crap after eating, and ravenous after dieting. You name the form of exercise, I hated it — gym, yoga, walking or cycling! I always felt like a failure. Despite being loved by those closest to me, they always hoped I would lose weight. All the while, I did not have the capacity to fully understand how to fully know myself or really understand my own feelings. All I could do was eat my way through it all.

Somewhere in my late 20s and early 30s, I got tired. The way I was living my life was not going to work. I knew it. I was beginning to feel the fatigue of constantly being at war inside myself. It came to a point where I could not function like a pendulum swinging from binge-eating to fasting. But I had not quite given myself the opportunity to access the tools that could support me in breaking free from these patterns, and to therefore form a healthy and intelligent relationship with myself. I had no idea how to begin to understand and love myself beyond losing weight. My society and culture had informed so much of my self-knowledge, that I did not know how to go beyond that. I simply did not know how to have a different experience of myself in my body or how to change conflicting self-talk such as, "You're so cute and adorable, just lose some weight!"

During this time, I found *Persicope*, a live-streaming video application. Like a prayer answered from above, on one not-so-ordinary night, a notification popped up on my phone. I sleepily clicked on it at 10:00pm and up popped a woman who looked a bit like me, unapologetically dancing in a room. She was sharing prompts on how to move our bodies. At that moment, I felt liberated just by looking at her. I felt if she can dance, so can I. Later that week, I reached out to Sara and asked more about the movement practice. This is how I found Qoya, a movement practice that I now teach.

Qoya is based on the idea that when women move, we remember our essence and Qoya describes this essence as wise, wild, and free[2]. The next day I connected with Sara and signed up for a package that included receiving individual movement videos. Ironically, Sara had never offered this package to anyone else. It was as if it was made for me. I received six videos and I danced to all of them, every day for six months. As each day came, I was able to let go of my limiting narrative around my body and expand deeper into truly knowing myself. I still remember all of the songs in the videos. They were sweetly chosen so I could lovingly and brutally unshackle myself. I remember playing the song, *My Body Is a Jail*, the Arcade Fire version, and the words allowed me to explore

---

[2] www.qoya.love

what it felt like in my body to feel limited and restricted, but without feeling guilty or like a failure. In doing so, I liberated myself from the "body-jail" I had created inside myself by defining myself by the opinions of others.

I began to set myself free. Movement became my answer. To be able to move every day to songs like *Break the Shell* by India Arie, with lyrics that allowed me to experience my truth and free my *Divine Nature* to come through, ray by ray.

Here's what I want to share with you: there are some fundamental thoughts you are holding onto about who you are, that hold you back from being *all* you can be.

People around you may pass judgement about you, around what they find acceptable or not. Maybe your parents said something at the dining table, or your grandparents. Maybe at a Thanksgiving dinner, an uncle or aunt pointed something out about you and everyone laughed, and it's remained with you since. Maybe it was high school friends who decided one day to tease you over something. Maybe these comments and remarks have hit you so hard that you have adopted and internalised them as truth and are holding on to them. These opinions may now define you. They certainly may have slowed you down in life and made you feel unworthy and unimportant. Perhaps they have made you feel that you are not needed and are just an "extra".

Today I want to share with you that another person's judgement of you is *NOT* your truth. Their reflection (judgement) is actually a projection of their insecurities and is *NOT* your truth.

Judgement binds you.

The opinions of others restrain you.

The more you play it in your mind, the more you begin to believe it.

The more you believe it, the more you want to hold on to it. This becomes your safe zone.

And your mind-body-heart narrative revolves around holding that judgement up as your truth.

So, as you grow older,

The more you begin to undermine yourself.

The more you begin to underestimate yourself.

The more you begin to strip yourself away from the life you are meant to lead.

What will it take for you to break free?

What will it take for you to look at every limiting, restrictive comment that anyone has ever said about you and throw it out? Dismiss it, trash it, get rid of it. Unburden and unleash yourself. So, you can begin to listen to your Inner Intelligence, your inner compass, your intuition and the voice of your spirit.

How would it feel in your body if you could let that limiting thought go? How would it feel in your body if you could say *Yes!* to the niggling feeling that whispers every day to you, telling you that you are more than what the gossip has said you are?

My niggling voice said to me: "You do not need to be fixed." My body reverberates to this day, with the memory of having felt that, around age ten. At that point, I did not know how to give more space to that voice to blossom inside me. Instead, it remained silent for decades.

The only way to change your narrative is to write a new one, to let your inner voice have a chance. Movement allowed me that space — space to find a new perspective and stop looking at myself the way others had taught me to look. Instead, that space allowed for a new perspective, one that was always present. It was mine and I practised embodying that a little more each day. With this came new words to fill my vocabulary. The truth is that the more I moved, the deeper sense of good I felt in my body. My body no longer felt like a barrier, a prison, a block. It transformed into being a vessel for my truth and to flow, as I re-acquainted myself with what it meant to be me; to be in a big body and to love me as I am.

Here's what I know now about the society we live in. Judgement is always at play. As kids, we're told we are not worthy until we conform; until we make ourselves acceptable. Society teaches you who you need to be before you can even begin to understand who you are. Further, that to be loved has a cost. Sometimes you pay by losing yourself. You spend years trying to fix, conform and "live appropriately" by those judgements. In the process, you abandon your spark, your dynamism and your vivaciousness.

My vision for you is to step away from these limiting constructs. There is a bigger, better world that you can create and magnetise towards yourself. Only once you step into owning and embracing all of who you are and begin listening to your voice.

I travelled all the way from India to Costa Rica to meet Sara and take my first full Qoya class. I found women there who celebrated me because I celebrated myself. Women who honoured me because I honoured myself. I found a community. I found a sense of belonging; a place I created and built because I dared to change the way I saw myself.

I am now a Qoya teacher and co-host Qoya retreats and share Qoya across the world. I work with women across the globe, sharing ideas of creating joy-full-ness, ease and freedom in our bodies and life.

Judgement creates patterns of action.

Patterns that deprive you of knowing yourself.

Patterns that hold you back from experiencing yourself.

Patterns that are unhealthy.

Patterns that do not serve you.

Patterns that are not yours to embody.

Patterns that keep you feeling small.

Patterns that make you feel helpless.

It is time you recognise your patterns. They're present as a result of believing and upholding the insecurities of people around you, so they may feel comfortable. Once you know your patterns, you can begin falling out of them.

Qoya allowed me to see the patterns I had created. My journey to creating new ones began from the sheer remembering that my body size does not define me, it is not my story. It was a judgement in my life that I trashed and burnt. I threw away the idea that I needed to "fix" myself to feel worthy. My disconnect with my body caused me to overeat throughout my life and hate the idea of forming a positive, healthy relationship with myself. As I continue to dismantle the judgments of others from my life, I create space for renewed, positive action.

The judgement of others is "trash-able", "get rid-able" and "do away with-able". You can live without it. You can survive without it. In fact, you may even thrive in its absence, because you can lift yourself up. You can find a new path for yourself and you can bring that voice (your inner guidance) to lead the way. It is possible.

How can you remember your *Self*? What can you do after you acknowledge that a lot of what you believe as truth about you, isn't actually yours?

Your journey of remembering the Truth about you, i.e., what you see, witness, acknowledge, celebrate and honour about yourself through thought and action on a daily basis, will come from a place that best supports you. Exploring avenues of expression such as movement; singing; different mediums of art (such as clay, colour or paper); or returning to nature (connecting with sand on a beach; twigs and rocks near a riverbed; or fallen leaves in a forest) will all provide space for a breakthrough. These mediums of letting the subconscious be expressed will provide you a portal that will help you recognise the parts of yourself that, although essential, are missing in your life. Find an avenue that allows you to enshrine your spirit back in your body. Give yourself space to dismantle the old so the new can be born inside of you.

One tip I'd like to share here is to recognise your portal as one that is easily accessible to you daily. Just as movement is accessible to me — I dance to a song every single day. The best part is, I now know women who do it with me! That's what happens when you begin to return to yourself as well as see yourself for the brilliance you are, you naturally find and connect with people who follow a similar path in life.

Just like attending a workshop or a class, there are a few things you must bring to your choice of empowered practice — be that movement, song, art or other. In order to help you to remember and embrace your truth, and confidently stand in your body, offer your unconditional love, kindness, and presence to this sacred practice. You cannot do this work if you place yourself second. You cannot commit to a journey of remembering your brilliance and the recognition of your *Spirit* by not showing up fully (or only showing up when it is convenient).

This journey is full of ups and downs. Not all days are the same and there will be slip-ups, and what I like to call the occasional *Cha-Cha-Cha* — meaning you take two steps forward, one step back. Or, on some days ... one step forward, three steps back! There will be days where you are grateful for the work you are doing to build this new life. You will be excited by the prospect of a new day, bursting forth with ideas on how to implement new actions. Yet, there will be days you'll want to give up. There might be a time when a comment from someone you love will bring you down, or when you will be threatened by people as they wield their weapon of conditional love. You will think it is pointless, and that it's better to go back to the life you had. Know, that the road may get lonely.

Through all of these times, your *Why* will carry you through. It will help you re-emerge and recommit, as well as help you to stay on purpose when you slip back. Some return to the work days, months or even years later.

Your *Why* is what brings you *Joy* (or the emotion you feel when you set yourself free). *Joy* comes as you express yourself fully. There is a part of you that longs to be seen, heard, felt and most importantly, *expressed*. The more you step into the fullest expression of you, the more (insert your preferred emotion here) you will feel for having said *Yes!*

My commitment to creating a healthy, honest and transparent relationship with my body is important to me. I desire to be a fully expressed human being. I desire to travel the world, share my work and sit in a circle with you talking about how we create our life with purpose and passion. I do not want to die never having experienced and relished all aspects of my *Spirit*, This is my *Why*. On days I feel lonely, or months after straying from my path — disheartened, almost willing to quit — I remind myself why this journey is so important to me. The *Joy* I feel brings me back, slowly, kindly and with ease and grace.

Your *Why* will do the same for you. It is always present, always ready to guide you and to hold your hand as you gently navigate a new path, so that you can begin to experience all the different aspects of your multidimensional *Spirit*. Remember, your journey is as a human *Being*. and by *Being* on this new path, you give yourself the opportunity to explore your *All-ness* just a little deeper. So, you can be a fully *Soul-Driven, Spirit-Expressed Human Being*. Now that is a beautiful thing. It is divine, it is magnetic and it is liberation. It is being *ALIVE*.

Your Gift

Radzy is offering readers who wish to join me in Embody Your Brilliance; A 12-week journey with Radzy to help you stand in your full expression and embody all of who you are. There is great joy, freedom and ease as you begin to experience and express all of who you are in this world. Open yourself to new beginnings, opportunities, possibilities and say YES to creating your life with purpose and direction that fuels you.

In this course, you will receive weekly emails from Radzy with journal prompts, movement suggestions, and other tools and techniques to support you in coming home to yourself in your body. To participate, please write to Radzy at radzychugh@gmail.com

facebook.com/radzychugh/

instagram.com/radzy_chugh/

www.fuelledbyjoy.com

FAYE HARTLEY-YOUENS

Being an empowered woman literally means to impart power to someone who lacks it. It is given and not claimed. That pretty much is against the essence of feminism. I strongly believe that women have always been strong and, therefore, cannot be empowered. The strength is right within them and has always been. All they need to do is tap into their innermost femininity and nourish it.

Faye is a clinical hypnotherapist, mind performance coach and the owner of Mind Performance Excellence. Faye works with athletes, performers (arts), business leaders and entrepreneurs to improve their performance both professionally and personally. Faye comes from a solid background of empowering women to live free from fear, anxiety and self-limiting beliefs.

www.mindperformanceexcellence.com

faye@mindperformanceexcellence.com

CARMEN SMITH

Carmen is an online business coach who often works with passionate, driven women looking to unleash their potential, create their own financial independence and live a life by their design!. Carmen is passionate about helping women thrive in life with more passion and self-belief to be their fully expressed selves with more purpose in our day to day lives. Carmen is an avid horse owner, equine competitor and nature lover, always looking to surround herself with other empowered women, sunsets, mountains and waterways.

THE COURAGE IN BECOMING ME

I think I watched too many Disney movies growing up. The prince always seemed to sweep in and save his princess and live happily ever after. However, that didn't seem to happen in my life. I travelled overseas during my 20s, through America and Europe. I studied Natural Horsemanship, which is about building a relationship with horses. Its studying a form of communication, understanding the natural psychology of the horse, learning about their body language they use to communicate with each, then applying this in our human world to interact with them on the ground or riding. I worked my way towards my dream job of becoming a Natural Horsemanship Instructor.

My Dad would often say to me, "If you love what you do, you'll never work a day in your life!"

First thing out of school, I went to work for Mum and Dad in our family real estate office for five years. My Dad loves Real Estate, its in his blood, I think he was secretly hoping I'd have this same love affair. I had a love-hate relationship with an office job. I didn't want to work inside. I didn't want to wear a dress to work every day, but I did it for education, for experience and because it was our family business. So, I did this until 2000, when my dad was diagnosed with oesophageal cancer. Our whole world got flipped upside down by his illness, and we were quickly reminded of what is important in life! For me, that was to follow my own heart and dreams.

And so, after Dad's huge operation and once he was given the "all clear", Mum gave me the nudge needed to begin living my own dream. I wanted to pursue a career in the horse industry. In 2001, I left all that I knew behind and ventured off on my own to university some 1,500 kilometres away to begin living my dream of working with horses. After graduating from university, more doors opened for me. My "horse dream" took me all over the world, working and studying Natural Horsemanship, holidaying and living the good life! I worked hard in a relatively male-led leadership team. I was doing the work of long nights, early mornings and little pay. Dreams were achieved and then replaced with bigger dreams. I then returned to Australia in 2009, set myself up and ventured out teaching natural horsemanship. I got myself a horse; a truck and a horse-trailer and began travelling around Australia teaching weekend clinics.

I was on the road for six to eight months of the year, travelling six to ten hours per day with horse and dog in tow. It was my dream life — the gypsy, the fiery-soul woman that longed to keep moving her feet and experiencing life; the horses; the people; that lifestyle; and the beautiful Australian countryside. I also wore many hats: instructor; marketing guru; course designer; driver; horse-feeder and poo-picker-upper; set-up and pack-up crew; email responder; and finally, the calendar planner.

Everything was happening beautifully except for finances, the money to plan into the future or simply just to 'get ahead' wasn't happening. I kept making excuses ... for years. "You'll earn more income next year", I would tell myself hopefully. "It will be *my year* next year"; "It's a never-ending drought here in Australia, everyone is cutting back!" My clinic numbers were dwindling, and I wasn't reaching my own financial needs. I worked harder and put on more clinics each month. I gave up any spare time I had. I gave up my own hobbies. I drove further to reach more people, got busier and more exhausted, but didn't earn any more finances, just gained more debt. I worked myself to the ground, for 10 years I gave it my *all.*

And nothing changed. The emotional turmoil of watching the dream that I had worked so hard for over 17 years in total, come crashing down. That feeling that I couldn't make it work financially; that I was a failure; that if I was married things would be easier with two incomes. It was all just overwhelming! I worried that as I had no other skill-set and my backup plan of finding *Mr Right* was not happening, I was doomed. I remember a "line-in-the-sand" moment for me. Whilst teaching a workshop over the weekend, I was sitting in my horse-trailer all rugged-up from the freezing cold winter, thinking of how yet again I was not able to pay the bills. "Why am I working so hard and still not able to get ahead?" I gloomily asked myself. "Nothing changes if nothing changes Carmen," I answered back.

So, I began to look for something else. I applied for three part-time jobs at local Coles supermarkets. I didn't even get an interview! With my experience, I sent my resume out to a dozen real estate agencies in town. I was prepared to leave the horses, my dream and go back to real estate full-time. But nothing — not one response. It's these moments in life that build grit, determination and resilience. It always feels like rock bottom or that the sky is falling in. However, it's through these hardships that we find ourselves. We find our potential within because we are forced to dig deep.

And it was around this time that I noticed a friend on Facebook who I had never met, who was having great success with an online business. With me having no experience in the online world, I reached out to see if it was something I could learn. I watched a webinar that offered to teach me a skillset that would enable me to grow my own personal brand, through an educational platform affiliated with products in the health & wellness sector. I was curious to learn more. I started to meet other amazing women, from all different backgrounds. All of them creating amazing success for themselves financially. They were creating an impact in their own lives, their family's and other people's lives too. They had gained back time for themselves to follow their passions and enjoy life creating more memories. I didn't want to do networking parties, I didn't want to cold call or message family & friends to ask them to buy my products, I didn't want to work hard for little return. I desired time freedom and financial independence for myself, I desired this with all my being, but I was hugely scared. Scared of failure. Scared that it might be a scam and scared of other people's opinions. I was also scared of losing the little money that I did have left. Scared of starting something new at 39 years old. But it was also just as scary to stay stuck in the same place, in my excuses; to stay stuck in the same industry that I couldn't make work; and to stay stuck in my own fear and scarcity. It reminded me of a quote, "Fear kills more dreams than failure ever will" by Suzy Kassem in her book, *Rise Up and Salute the Sun: The Writings of Suzy Kassem.*

By this stage, my self-worth and confidence was at an all-time low. Being in a male-dominated leadership team for the last few years, it was all about the *doing* to get ahead that comes with masculine work, *always hustling, always doing, working harder.* My voice was constantly drowned out and falling on deaf ears. I began to feel there was little value in speaking up. "You're too emotional Carmen," the voices said "You're too loud!", "You're too much!". So, I shrank. I hid. I played small, to blend in and not to rock the boat.

The quote by Albert Einstein kept repeating in my ear, "We cannot solve our problems with the same thinking we used when we created them." I needed to move through my own fears and excuses related to succeeding in the online business space. If these other women could create this for themselves, then why not me? And in addition to learning this skill set of affiliate marketing, the educational platform dived into inner personal development work too. It included trainings around growing my self-worth; my money mindset; my confidence and my belief in myself. We spend the most amount of time with ourselves in our lives, so why not become our own biggest cheer-squad? Why not back ourselves and believe that we can achieve what we set out to? What if we talked to ourselves like we would our best friend?

And so, I dived in full of fear, excitement and what if. What if this would totally change my life. What if this was everything I had been asking the universe for. Step number one on my journey of starting my online business was to read the book, *The Magic* by Rhonda Byrne. This book changed my life. It introduced me to a morning ritual for myself, filled with gratitude and journaling. I've always been a grateful person, but this book helped me understand actual embodiment of deep gratitude. It taught me how to manifest our own desires and create a morning journaling ritual that created time and space to nurture and grow myself. It showed me how to share my fears, my doubts and create the abundance I was calling into my life.

Our capacity to love others is only limited by our capacity to love and hold *ourselves*. I truly needed to fall in love with myself again, to remember who I was. Not the fear and labels that myself or others had placed on me. And it starts with the inner work. It starts by slowing down and remembering our feminine power within. The truth that, "Your outer world reflects your inner world", was a hard "truth-pill" for me to swallow as my outer world was a mess. I craved more loving human relationships, but equally craved my own time alone. I was confident and certain on the outside, but heaven forbid a piece of the puzzle moved because I would come crashing down. There wasn't much holding me up, and I feared the fall. I was afraid of what people would think of me building a personal online brand! I decided that building a personal brand was only based around *me* and my values and beliefs and so, would naturally attracts others with similar beliefs and values. Secondly, I decided everyone has opinions just like elbows and arseholes, and they wouldn't pay my bills, so best I get over that quickly!

And so, as I dived into the mindset training and embodiment training, the calibre of presenters impressed me and I started to feel myself growing and changing. I started to remember who I was and the potential that was inside of me. I started seeing things magically appear in my world that I had been journaling around. Magically $3,500 appeared in my account from a supplier finding money owed to me, store discounts, bank refunds, tax refunds - I was amazed what started coming my way! Relationships started to blossom and my energy levels had me bounding out of bed in the morning!

111

Now I found myself surrounded by a beautiful tribe of powerful women inviting me forward into this area of life and business. I had created a vision that was in my heart that I was now working towards bringing to life. My vision in the beginning, was to create financial independence and time freedom to enjoy life again! I wanted to save myself and then to help others create the same in their life. Sure, I ran into a handful of *Negative Nancies* or cautious people that believed that network marketing was all a scam. I did not let their fears dictate my dreams. I worked hard for over 17 years following societies mould, go to uni, get a job, get a promotion, buy a house, work really hard and repeat till you retire. I couldn't make it work financially — that was the real scam! I was not going to settle.

My business started gaining traction and I created my first five-figure income online within the first few months. This blew my mind entering with no experience. I dedicated five to seven hours each week to my online brand. I juggled this passion project part-time around my then full-time job. I educated myself on new skills and I was now reaping the rewards. I could feel the success brewing! My vision grew as I grew, and I began mentoring other women to unleash their voice - their personal brand, reach their potential and create financial independence for themselves!

It was also around this time that I considered having a baby and began to research travelling down the In-Vitro-Fertilization (IVF) path. I had been thinking about it for a while, procrastinating and probably fearful of not having the time or finances to raise a family. I allowed fear to rule my life and now I was slowly taking the reins back in these areas. I hadn't yet met *Mr Right* or even *Mr Wrong,* but I wanted to start a family. I wasn't going to rush into something quickly or sit around waiting. So, I dived into the huge journey that IVF is. There were months of different appointments; counselling; finding donors that matched with my DNA quirks; waiting for new donors; and then more appointments. All these take time, and so I was appreciative of this new time freedom I had gained by working in the online space.

After a 12-month journey, at 40 years of age, everything aligned and the daily hormone injections began along with internal scans every few days to see how things were progressing. Then egg retrieval date was set. It was exciting and daunting all at the same time. I had 21 eggs collected, which I was over the moon about, followed by fertilising the eggs. By day five I had two remaining embryos. The emotional rollercoaster continued. How could this be? The doubt set in. "What if this doesn't work, there's only two embryos left?" I began to doubt & worry. Luckily by then, I had gained mindset tools through my online business trainings, that would serve me for the inner work I would need to practice.

The next month's date was set for implantation. It was a bit of a non-event really and two-weeks later I received the positive news that I was pregnant! It was so exciting to hear the news and feel yet another dream coming to life. I had created time and financial freedom that made starting a family possible. I could easily work from home in the pockets of time I had. It felt like it was all coming together. I found myself at a cross-road. Should I dedicate more time towards my online business and cut back on teaching hours? My heart screamed *Yes!* So, I made the next leap and halved my teaching commitments over the next few months so that I could create business online from home. This afforded less travel and more time for growing a vegetable garden; local yoga classes; lunch with friends; riding my own horses and pursuing my own passions.

My first-year anniversary in the online space was approaching, and along with celebrating this huge milestone, I also got to celebrate creating a six-figure-income business. I had totally replaced my teaching income in my first 12 months. The shy and quiet woman, who was filled with doubt and uncertainty, had risen as a courageous, certain and worthy woman who was now leading others to bring their own visions to life in the online space. I was still enjoying teaching horsemanship clinics, but more from love than needing to reach monthly finances.

However, not all was rosy. As life goes, it was on one of my trips to Cairns in Northern Queensland, Australia, that I went in for a nine-week ultrasound. It was there that I was told I had a missed miscarriage. The emotional pain of coming to terms with the news, being told what the next medical steps would be and dealing with the outside world, was a whirlwind. Why me? Why now? A dream I thought would come to life, came crashing down in a moment. I spent weeks hiding from the outside world, and the pain of seeing every pregnant woman or baby that had become a heart stabbing reminder. I did try several months later with the second embryo to fall pregnant again, but it wasn't to be either. I sat with this for months, asking myself if I wanted to venture down this avenue again. I decided I didn't want to. This time, not based on fear, but based on my desire to trust that the universe had my back. I decided instead to spend my energy creating a loving relationship with myself and in turn a special man, who was coming into my life. Gabby Bernstein's book *Super Attractor* was a great guiding path in this decision.

And so, I focused on my own mental and emotional healing. I read more books around *feminine strengths* and *doing the work* to rid limiting beliefs that were holding me back. Then, I focused my energy on creating and nurturing things in my life: relationships and business. I watched my life flourish. When we step out of the shadows that hold us back, when we remove the upper limits blocking our success, we give ourselves permission to shine and in turn, give others permission too.

Fast forward three years, and not only has my mindset and my self-worth grown enormously, my business has surpassed one-million Australian dollars in sales. It has allowed me to thrive in my own areas of passion. It has supported me to create time and financial independence for myself, whilst mentoring other women to create this for themselves too.

In the end, I got to save myself. Instead of waiting for someone else to save me. That's what I'm proud of! I'm proud of the woman who has emerged along this journey, and excited for the next evolution emerging.

Your Gift

The hardest person you'll ever have to walk away from is the person you've become, to step into the person you're becoming. This has been one of my greatest lessons to date. And on the other side of this, was also my greatest achievement, of the woman I stepped into being. I mentor many women worldwide to unleash their potential and step into their fully expressed selves, to leverage an online business platform around their lifestyle of family & kids or horses, hobbies and work.

If you're looking to learn more about unleashing your potential & leveraging digital marketing, go to my website below and download my free book that can help show you how.

Connect with Carmen

www.abundancewithcarmen.com

JEANNE RUSSELL

I think an empowered woman is a woman that is free to be herself. Where she has come to that point in her life where she is free to express herself openly and honestly. A point where she has realized who she is and is not afraid to let the world see her beauty, her essence, her passion, her anger, her joy, her sorrows-to fully embrace all parts of herself without permission!

The fact is we are all empowered women. It's our biological right being down here in this 3-D reality to be empowered, have what we want, do what we want, and say what we want. We had it as a child. Somewhere along the way, we lost this freedom. Look at the children and learn by their example. Look at how they act. They don't hold back. They are themselves in every moment, sometimes demanding, sometimes joyful for no reason, and sometimes sad and will not be consoled.

But what happens? We become what is expected of us. We act as we think others want us to act. We do what we think others want us to do. And in the process, we lose ourselves—our sense of self.

So my question to you is, will you have the courage to be yourself, to embrace the true you that is begging to come through? Will you let society and outside influences mould and shape you, or will you be true to yourself, true to your heart, and fully embrace the beautiful, powerful, and enlightened woman you came here to be? Yes, it takes courage. Yes, it may be difficult at times. Yes, old friends may drop away. No one said this journey was going to be easy. But I can promise you this. It will be a life fulfilled and one that you will be proud to share with your children and everyone who knows you. So make your choice. There is no right or wrong, but I have made mine, and I would delight in sharing this adventure with you! Mahalo.

Jeanne Marie Russell is the Owner of the Dolphin Touch Wellness Center located in Kauai, Hawaii. She is a Reiki Master/Teacher, Retreat Facilitator, Realtor, and Creator of Dolphin Energetics(R), a healing modality devoted to the energy and vibration of the dolphin. She facilitates Online Intuitive Reiki Training and Lemurian Retreats in Kaua'i, Hawaii.

www.DolphinTouch.org

NICOLLE EDWARDS

Nicolle Edwards is the Founder and Chief Executive Officer of RizeUp Australia, a not-for-profit providing practical support to families fleeing domestic and family violence. In partnership with specialist domestic and family violence services, RizeUp provides groundbreaking practical support to families impacted by domestic and family violence. As families traverse the journey from danger to safety, RizeUp walks alongside them to create safe, bright, new beginnings. From creating fully furnished homes and providing vital resources for children beginning again at new schools to covering the cost of specialist counselling and medical support, RizeUp is an instrumental piece of the trauma recovery puzzle.

Described as a velvet sledgehammer, Nicolle is generous, direct, warm, engaging and supportive. Nicolle has a sales and marketing background, but her passion for charity work began in 2012 after setting up a house for a woman who had left her violent relationship. Nicolle's journey has been widely recognised by the community; she is an accomplished TEDx speaker, podcast guest, Westfield Hero twice over and Commonwealth Games 2018 Queen's Baton Relay bearer, to name a few.

As the 2017 recipient of the Excellence in Volunteer Management Award (Queensland Volunteering Awards), Nicolle currently manages over 750 volunteers. She is resolute in expanding RizeUp across Australia and New Zealand.

To find out more about RizeUp, please visit www.rizeup.com.au

COURAGE

"Everyone deserves to be safe."

I pay respect to all victim-survivors of domestic and family violence, and I honour your courage and determination.

I see you. I believe you. I stand with you.

In the spirit of reconciliation, I also acknowledge the Traditional Custodians of Country throughout Australia and their deep connections to land, sea and community. I pay my respect to their Elders, past and present. I extend that respect to all Aboriginal and Torres Strait Islander peoples.

When thinking about what I could write for this chapter, I considered my drive and what has ultimately driven me to lean into the space of domestic and family violence. So much happens in our lives. I often think about how each decade makes a chapter in the book that is ultimately our life. If we look hard enough, a constant theme runs throughout; like a ribbon intricately weaving our metaphorical pages together. As the ribbon intertwines through our lives, it can become tangled. Sometimes we lose the end, but as we turn each page every day, we eventually re-find the ribbon. We then continue to thread.

Since I was little, I have always felt passionately about speaking up, challenging things that seemed unfair. Whether it was the new girl at school who arrived from overseas with the 'funny' accent or other contentious issues, I usually had something to say about it, from bullying and racial injustice to domestic and family violence. These social issues impelled me to follow the ribbon of injustice. To have the courage to speak out and challenge oppression.

So how about we go right back to the beginning?

I was born in Zimbabwe. My family comprised of my Mum, Dad, brother, and I. Due to political unrest, we all moved to Durban, South Africa. It wasn't until 1985 that we crossed the great Indian Ocean to get to Australia.

One of my earliest memories involves a buffet breakfast, served with a side of piping hot discrimination. I was maybe five or six years old, and my family and I were on holiday. It was breakfast time, and I remember the chocolate brown booth that my brother Brett and I had slid into. I remember the enormous array of delicious buffet breakfast food. A feast before my eyes; hot breakfasts were my favourite. I couldn't wait to pile up my plate with as much as I was allowed.

As my mom and dad settled into the booth alongside us, my attention landed on a tall African man. He was waiting in line with the other diners. I remember his skin was as dark as night, and his smile was easy and at the ready. What happened next has stayed with me my whole life. Nearby diners began making fun of him under their breath but loud enough for me to hear.

At six years old, I didn't understand much about race, nor the challenges faced by many. What I recognised was a strange feeling in my tummy like a fire. I was mad. It didn't make sense to me. Why were they being so mean?

I have come to recognise that feeling. It burns when I face injustices of any kind. It was a ribbon that would weave through my life; at six years old, I became an activist against injustice.

Looking over the last 40 years, I can identify a pattern of my behaviour, of speaking out when people aren't treated equitably. However, one incident in particular ultimately changed the course of my life and led me to where I am now, the founder of RizeUp Australia.

It was a lovely September afternoon. I was contacted to help a woman (let's call her Ava) who had made quite a journey to arrive on the Gold Coast, Australia. During that time, she gathered her four children, jumped on a train, and headed out for a 'quick lunch'. What was significant, though, was that this wasn't just any train trip or lunch date. They were escaping. Ava had little more than her handbag, a small backpack, her eight-month-old baby and three older children. She packed down her fear, gathered all the courage she could muster, and jumped on a cross-country train from Perth to the Gold Coast. They had one chance; this was going to have to be it.

Ava hadn't taken anything else, that fateful day. To do so would have alerted the person committing horrendous violence against her and her children. She had been planning her escape for months and had tried so many times before to leave, but it had been too dangerous. The repercussions were devastating. Finally, the day had come, and she knew that she had to leave. The violence was beginning to escalate, and she may not have had another opportunity. The most shocking thing was that the person committing this terrible violence was the one person who should have been keeping her safe, respecting her and loving her; the man Ava had married eight years earlier and the father of her four children.

When I heard this story, all I could think was, how could this happen in our beautiful country? How could this woman feel so unsafe that her only option was to jump on a train and across the country, a distance of approximately 5263 kilometres, or five days of travelling?

Let's go back to Ava and give a little thought to what that would have been like for her. Five days, a small baby, three other children and one backpack. For those of you who are mums, can you imagine that? I'm a mum too, and I can't even fathom the level of desperation it would have taken to leave everything behind and journey that far with nothing more than a small bag, just to get to safety. Until that time, I'd never thought about domestic violence. It's not a subject that seemed to come up in conversations. But when I learned what Ava and her children had been exposed to, I felt enraged and shocked at the depravity and violations of human rights.

It was a massive injustice. How could I not get involved? With the help of my friends and family, we gathered as many supplies as we could. By the end of the first week, we had almost housed Ava and her children. What struck me so profoundly at the time was just how readily my community of friends and family jumped in to help. When we could turn around so quickly and do so much to support a family at risk, I knew that as a community, we could do even more for families experiencing similar situations. That was my lightbulb moment and we just needed to get started.

As with any new initiative, it hasn't been easy. The work I now do in the domestic and family violence advocacy space dropped into my lap almost ten years ago. There have been some pain points when my heart was broken, or I was betrayed. But, as the yogis might say, I've found my dharma, and I'm confident that I've been able to follow my life's true purpose.

The tricky thing about all this is how did I know that what I was doing was what I was meant to be doing? Why did I press through the pain points that took me through some of my darkest hours? And, most pressingly, how did I do it? Firstly, and most importantly, I can say that I didn't do it alone. Before I go any further,

I wanted to share with you my favourite African proverb. I think about it often, and it has become a bit of a motto for our RizeUp team. It goes something like this:

"If you want to go fast, go alone, but if you want to go far, go together."

I love that. If you want to achieve great things, you go together. There's another African word I love too, it's "Ubuntu". Have you heard that before? Essentially, it's the same as the proverb. Loosely translated, it means "I am, because you are". It's the collective way of thinking.

Apart from the benefits of connectivity, unity equals strength. Through collaborative thinking and a shared purpose, extraordinary things can be achieved. The ideas of others can inspire you to refine your purpose and further ignite the fire in your belly. A collective of like-minded changemakers can accomplish significant outcomes together. As the proverb states, the long race will be won if we go together.

Have you ever thought that maybe you too could be somebody who could make a big change? Could you be a changemaker?

Where (and how?) do we even begin to follow our passion? To the naked eye, the world looks mapped out. We can question whether we're equipped to make a change, if it's even worth trying. If change hasn't happened yet, does that mean that it's not going to happen?

When we consider pioneering a new idea, we become very aware of the negative discourse. These opposing views can be incredibly discouraging and can generate self-doubt. It takes enormous courage, but we have to believe in ourselves.

The first thing to remember is that our society is fluid and flexible. We can all be changemakers, no matter who we are, where we live, how much money we earn or what country we live in. We all have the capacity to be a part of something that can create positive outcomes for our community. We can all have the confidence to make the changes for a better, kinder society. In our way, we can connect to the potential we are each born with. However, life generally sees us switch to autopilot and become entrenched in the hustle and bustle of day-to-day life. We stop looking at things until we are reminded of our higher purpose when we cross paths with people like Ava.

For a change, there must be someone who has identified an idea or concept that can improve and add value to society. From there, for it to grow, develop, and harness momentum, we must then find our tribe, fellow agents for change who share the same passion, integrity, and purpose. The changemaker needs its community, and let's face it; we are social beings who work far better when we are interconnected and collaborating. A balanced, happy, and content life is challenging in isolation.

When we step into the change-making space, embrace what we want to do — and we're prepared to leave ownership and ego at the door — we launch ourselves into a journey of enormous self-discovery and immense gratitude. To be humble, honest, and driven to act from a space we have identified as our true north, we can create tremendous change. It's not easy stepping out into the light and out of our comfort zones. But to truly succeed, we need to recognise our potential. It's not just having the support of like-minded people, but confidence and courage to right wrongs, create a better world, and the ability to challenge precedents. What comes with that courage is that our lives can become enriched beyond measure by both the initiative and the amazing amount of like-minded people we encounter.

When we talk about the importance of coming together to see the creation of change, and we look back on history for examples - nowhere else will you see a greater coming together of people than when our society is faced with social injustice.

When I first heard about Ava and her children, apart from helping in an immediate and practical manner; I needed to learn more about domestic and family violence. I soon discovered that this intimate terrorism is as insidious as it is pervasive. Domestic and family violence is one of the most significant and undiscriminating social injustice issues in Australia and worldwide, affecting people from all races, religions, and social classes. The statistics are heartbreaking; we all must stand up and create the solution.

Key statistics on violence against women in Australia

(www.ourwatch.org.au)

- On average, one woman a week is murdered by her current or former partner.[1]

- 1 in 3 Australian women (30.5%) has experienced physical violence since the age of 15.[2]

- 1 in 3 Australian women (34.2%) has experienced physical and/or sexual violence perpetrated by a man since the age of 15.[4]

- 1 in 4 Australian women (23.0%) has experienced physical or sexual violence by a current or former intimate partner since age 15.[5]

- 1 in 4 Australian women (23.0%) has experienced emotional abuse by a current or former partner.[6]

- Australian women are nearly three times more likely than men to experience violence from an intimate partner.[7]

- Almost 10 women a day are hospitalised for assault injuries perpetrated by a spouse or domestic partner.[8]

- Intimate partner violence is the leading contributor to death, disability and ill-health in Australian women aged 15-44.

The impact and cost of violence against women

Violence against women takes a profound and long-term toll on women's health and wellbeing, on families and communities, and on society as a whole.

- In 2018-2019, Aboriginal and Torres Strait Islander females had 29 times the rate of hospitalisation for non-fatal family violence assaults when compared with non-Indigenous females.[19]

- Based on a 2015 analysis, violence against women in Australia costs Australia $21.7 billion each year.[20]

- Domestic or family violence is a leading driver of homelessness for women.[22]

Violence against women is an issue that affects those with children in their care. It can have ongoing and profound effects on the child's learning capacity, health, and emotional wellbeing. It also hinders their capacity for healthy, respectful relationships when they become adults. Children impacted by violence are at greater risk as adults of substance abuse issues, homelessness, and increased risk of suicidality.

Along with the tragic impact that violence has on the individual lives of women and their children, it also has community and economy-wide impacts. Sexual assault and domestic violence are the most common crimes in Australia.

All violence is wrong, regardless of the sex of the victim or perpetrator. However, there are distinct gendered patterns in the perpetration and impact of violence. Research shows us that Australia has a real problem with men's violence.

While men are more likely to experience violence by other men in public places, women are more likely to experience violence from men they know, and it's often in the home.

These statistics are shocking and why I am so passionate about the work we do at RizeUp to reinforce frontline agencies supporting families affected by domestic and family violence. RizeUp was created to drive awareness of domestic violence. There had to be some way to engage the broader community and drive home just how serious an issue we have with domestic and family violence in our country. No one talks about it, and no one wants to talk about it. We must address and challenge the drivers of intimate partner and family abuse to make significant changes to the cultural and societal issues that underpin attitudes allowing antisocial behaviour to continue.

RizeUp's primary focus is to reduce the incidence of domestic and family violence in Australia. At a practical level, and without ever meeting, we support families impacted by violence by helping them on their journey from violence to safety. To do this successfully, we have created an innovative solution that brings communities together, increases volunteering and makes real, far-reaching and practical contributions to these vulnerable families. Stepping out of a violent relationship takes immense courage and inner strength and the knowledge that a community is waiting to support their decision to leave the violence behind.

As a family leaves refuge, our team of volunteers furnish their new accommodation with everything they need to make it a home. They can then make informed decisions to remain away from the violence. We also support affected children by providing everything they need to happily settle into a new school.

With hundreds of volunteers spread from coast to country, RizeUp Australia has become a vital part of the service system across Australia. It has established strong partnerships with specialist domestic violence services to provide fast, flexible solutions for families in desperate situations. Frontline services rely on RizeUp to help them safely transition victims/survivors of domestic and family violence from a life of fear and violence to one of safety and community. Our team is growing with incredible people from all walks of life across Australia.

From painters to CEOs to stay at home parents, we have the most incredible humans who each share a passion for altruism, the commitment to drive solutions, and the compassion to prioritise the challenges faced by those less fortunate than themselves.

I can't tell you how proud I am to be surrounded by people of this calibre. It warms my heart. I know that together we have created a legacy to help many, many women and children press restart for a life free from violence.

Regardless of whereabouts in the world we live, everyone can help prevent violence against women and children. We can start by holding our friends and family accountable for attitudes and behaviours. We can practice kind, respectful communication and ensure our microcosms are healthy. We can keep our eyes firmly planted where they should be: on those inflicting violence on the most vulnerable in their home. We need to stop asking, why doesn't she leave, and instead ask, why doesn't he stop hurting her?

RizeUp has become my anchor. Working alongside my husband, we often say, "we cannot unknow what we now know", and we have dedicated our lives to walk alongside the most vulnerable in our community. This journey is not ours alone, and the success of RizeUp is in no small part testimony to the strength of our team. The success of great feats relies heavily on those who walk alongside, who believe and are as invested and committed as you. As with many social justice issues, domestic and family violence is bigger than all of us together; it is so important to keep our eyes trained on reflective practice, enabling us to continue to create positive outcomes.

In the beginning, I was heartbroken. If it wasn't for the people around me, who remain around me to this day, I don't think I would have been able to get through it. It took me a little while to align with the right people who shared the same moral compass and whose kindness belied their fierceness and commitment to right a wrong. I've learnt some lessons along the way, and one of those lessons has been to trust my gut instinct.

Gosh, how many times do we have to hear that to believe it? If it doesn't feel right, it most likely isn't. I've learnt that, along with having passion, it's really important to choose your tribe carefully, courageously and unapologetically. If someone doesn't fit your vibe, it's ok. Don't force it. If it doesn't feel right, then it won't be right. It's very important that we give ourselves permission to back ourselves. Sometimes life can be cruel, and it puts people in your life to test you and to challenge your strength. This happens so often to so many people. There's no denying it's pretty awful, but you'll eventually get through it with a whole lot of lessons learnt and with even more courage.

In closing, I'd like to wish you all well. Always be kind, have integrity, and be passionate and considerate about those we share life's journey with. We only have one go at life, so we must give it our best. Change will come when we stay true to our convictions and surround ourselves with those who share our passions. By bringing happiness and kindness, our lives will be enriched with gratitude. Most of all, have courage to pursue what drives you.

Yours in service, reason and justice,

Nicolle

Nicolle Edwards | Founder and CEO | **RizeUp Australia**| (Pronouns: She/Her)

"No one is your friend who demands your silence or denies your right to grow."

~ Alice Walker

ROBYN ELLERBOCK

Robyn Is a passionate Love and Relationship Coach. She supports conscious women who are seeking a soulmate or who are currently in a relationship. To attract and create the kind of love and relationship experiences they deeply desire.

Robyn empowers women to activate their natural feminine energy and re-script their love story once and for all, for long term happiness and wellbeing in love.

Robyn is an expert in her field with over ten years of experience as a Life Coach. She has been featured in mum entrepreneur Magazine. Spotlighted in the Julie Lewin Academy Newsletter. Robyn was an ambassador for the global training. 'Art of feminine presence'. She holds qualifications as an NLP Coach, M- bit Coach and hypnotherapist.

In her free time, you can find her escaping into nature for walks and camping, or hanging out with her hubby and three daughters, usually drinking chai tea!

How I Chose Myself And Reclaimed A Loving Relationship

Along the journey of discovering her power, there comes a time in every woman's life where she inevitably needs to walk through her *Shadow of Darkness*. Unbeknownst to her at the time, the darkness greets her as a friend, calling her home to her beautiful wholeness. Though we do not know when this painful time will come. What really matters is that we understand how truly sacred the darkness is. There have been various times of darkness throughout my own life. The most significant one, which stayed the longest and had the greatest impact, was when I lost all sense of myself and the world around me.

My quiet life, at the time as a single parent of a 3-year-old daughter, had abruptly changed. I was recently back together, living with my high-school sweetheart after three significant years apart, our relationship was unexpectedly much more strained and difficult than I could have imagined; I had just given birth to twin girls. One of our daughters was born with a chronic illness, and in her first week of life, she had narrowly avoided brain-damage from extremely high jaundice levels. After receiving immediate care, she was finally able to come home to us. I was suddenly struck with the overwhelming fear and responsibility of keeping her alive on my own, away from medical assistance.

Everything in my life seemed out of my control, including how I was feeling day to day, sometimes even minute to minute. It took me back to a time in my life where I had felt the same sense of everything being out of my control. My experience began one morning in my first year of school. I was unable to stand up as I got out of bed. For some reason, my right leg would not work. My mum reassured me that my leg was numb from having slept on it all night.

That following night I was violently ill, and the next day I was admitted into hospital. Doctors tried to stop an infection that had taken hold in the deep tissue of my right leg and in so doing, they had saved my life. The doctors sought to find out exactly how my leg had become so severely infected.

I remember one morning lying in the hospital bed, listening to the doctors and specialists, during an awaited conversation about my prognosis. I caught pieces of their conversation, "We may have to amputate ... it might be the only option!" I worried about what would happen if my leg was amputated. I asked myself, *what would my life look like? How could anyone love me? Who would be my friend if I couldn't walk or play with them?* I lay there paralysed in fear. I'm ashamed to admit that at that moment, I felt dying might be a better option. Luckily, I did recover fully. I learned to walk again. However, I carried the heavy physical and emotional scars that were left after my hospitalisation. The doctors never discovered what happened to my leg, and the cause of the infection remains a mystery to this day.

I was now experiencing a new time of overwhelm as a young mother in a strained relationship, where all these earlier fears resurfaced. *Who could love me as I am?* These painful stories plagued me daily and I found them to be reflected like a giant mirror. Most strongly in my disconnected intimate relationship at the time, which was the very place I yearned to feel secure and loved. I did not see them for what they were at the time; old stories and fears needing to be healed and released. I saw them as foolproof truths about myself; that had to be shamefully hidden. I felt stuck, alone, and desperate to feel safe within myself.

In life, I have discovered if one does not bravely turn towards the doubt and shame (that is really a friend disguised as darkness), one will inevitably keep experiencing its shadow. In other words, one will somehow repeat the painful experience until the teaching and healing is embraced. I was unable to see that

I was making every choice in my life from a place of fear and insecurity. All the while, deeply desiring to feel free. I held tight to a destructive belief that if I were perfect enough, I would be loved. The expectation of perfection was my driving force but also my last fearful grasp at hope.

Due to my declining self-worth, I found myself face down on a surgery operating table in the hospital. I was desperately hoping some reconstructive surgery would erase my childhood story and the road map that led me to the surgery table that day. Though in a sacred twist of fate, the medical professional in which I had placed all my trust, caused much physical agony and then created a greater mess of my leg. I was paralysed on the surgical table in terror. My mind began to race with fear. Only this time, I was not wondering, *Who could love me like this?* Or *maybe it would be better if I died.* Instead, my terror was, *I might die right here, right now.* All I could think of was my family at home, my kids and my partner. How could I leave them like this? What on earth was I doing here? In a desperate search for love, I had shut myself out. I had shut out love. I realised I might not feel lovable, but I had so much love to experience and give! This time, paralysed in fear again just as I was as a child, I chose life. I chose myself, just as I was, for better or worse. And so began my journey to true love and freedom.

The hardship that followed this experience was immense. It was filled with guilt, panic attacks, grief, and deep depression. It was however, the uphill journey back home to myself that I needed. I was willing and ready to do the work and to greet the darkness with courage in my heart. There were so many desires birthed from this difficult time. I wished to be the best mother I could be. I yearned to be in a beautiful, loving and conscious relationship. I desired greatly to support others to find their way in the dark too.

So, how does one begin to heal? There is no right way to heal other than turning inwards and allowing our hearts to lead. To lead us to what feels right at each new stage of healing and growth. For me, I understood that I needed to rescue myself in order to uncover my power source as a woman. It was clear; no one was coming to save me, No strong man. No amount of self-imposed perfection or outside sources had ever been the answer. So, my healing journey began with reclaiming my inner child.

I soaked up John Bradshaw's book *Home Coming: Reclaiming and Championing Your Inner Child.* Whilst reading it, I had so many revelations. The book helped me realise why I was insecure, plagued with feelings of never mattering to others and feeling so unlovable. I dedicated my time to every exercise within those pages that he recommended. To my surprise, as I turned inward, my inner child awaited me there. I discovered she was proud of me and the choices I had made. This was a breakthrough moment for me. I found I was not failing and all bad. I was doing much better than I had believed. John Bradshaw, through his book, walked me through every stage of healing myself from trauma and abandonment to understanding my own needs. He was the guiding father figure I never had.

With this, my quality of mothering grew tremendously. I found myself immersed in author Louise Hay's work on affirmations. I began teaching her work to my children and in turn started classes for other children. I wanted everyone to understand the power of their thoughts and how we create our reality with our beliefs! Positive Affirmations became a daily practice in my life. However, as the rest of my life was healing, piece by piece, my relationship with my partner was still under strain. My desire for great love and connection was a constant driver in my life. Now that I had grown so much myself, I was able to turn my focus to learning and discovering my inner power in my intimate relationship. Through attending Imago Relationship Therapy, developed by Dr Harville Hendrix and Dr Helen LaKelly Hunt, I learned relationships mirror our unresolved childhood wounds. I learned that we play out unresolved issues in our intimate partnerships. All the hurts we experienced as children; all the places we were unable to get our love-needs met by our primary carers. I learned our partners will often replicate a similar trait or quality to that of our primary caretakers, triggering a pattern of painful powerlessness.

My partner and I discovered that the first step to a conscious relationship, was to understand each other's experience of love growing up. This insight into understanding each other's triggers, and different ways of feeling loved, was so important in our journey. The other gift we gained was to shift our focus to a positive connection and create a foundation of loving, trusting communication. We began a whole year of daily appreciations for one another. The impact of this practice was immense. I could see us both coming back to life with each word of love and praise from the other. I was beginning to feel so held and safe through our emotional intimacy, as we connected and appreciated one another again. But still in all this, there were patterns we could not easily resolve. These patterns would rear up and sabotage the connection and trust we had built up. This naturally took us down a path of feeling hopeless.

Eventually, in a moment of deep realisation I found the only way to create real change was to surrender the past inner wounds that no longer served our greatest vision of happiness. In letting go of control, we open ourselves up to new possibilities. We also activate our powerful re-birthing feminine energy as women. Marianne Williamson puts it eloquently, "The moment of surrender is not when life is over. It's when it begins."[3] In surrendering, my world opened. I started to receive so much wisdom and information about our sacred feminine energy. About what creates attraction and lasting love. I began learning the core qualities of healthy men and women. The transformation of love, between my partner and I, changed so rapidly! For the first time in my life I felt seen, valued,

[3] *Bradshaw (1992), Home Coming: Reclaiming and Championing Your Inner Child, Random House Publishing*
Marianne Williamson, RelicsWorld-A world of words which can change your life
Imago Relationship Therapy, Dr Harville Hendrix and Dr Helen LaKelly Hunt

adored and special. We finally began planning our wedding, after nearly two decades of struggling along. I felt like I had finally cracked the code. I had reached a stage where my heart felt lit-up in love, whilst still being deeply connected to my own power-source as a woman.

One of my most significant discoveries during this time was that men and women have vastly different qualities. The sexes I believe, have different ways of expressing, thinking, communicating and experiencing love. I believe it is our gift and responsibility to one another to discover and honour these core differences. I believe, we can come together as equal partners when combining our differences, as our individual strengths meet one another in unity.

My partner and I began a weekly meeting focused solely on the state of our relationship. We would start the meeting with a delicious appreciation of each other. Then we each took turns in sharing our thoughts, feelings and wishes. In actively listening, whilst following a therapy script, we began to truly hear one another. At last, we had landed on the same page. My husband tells me this is one of his most enjoyable times together. I have also become particularly good at leaning into my feminine energy and opening a space for my husband to meet my love needs. A woman having her needs met, is the most important element in feeling loved. We are deeply restored and brought back to our best, most colourful selves when our needs are met adequately and consistently.

If you were to take away only one thing from my story to support a thriving relationship, it would be to discover your own love needs and make a commitment to having them met. When a woman's heart opens in trust and love, she will light up for all to see. This is her greatest gift for the world. Through her divine radiance, a man will sense his true protective and devoted nature.

I once heard a relationship coach say that a relationship needs to have enough adventure to keep you interested. The example he used was a ski-run. He stated that if a ski-run is straight and predictable, you will not go back for more.

However, if it has just enough contrast, with bumps and turns, then you are likely to stay committed to the challenge. I wholeheartedly agree. I like to think of the challenges in our relationships as the grit in the oyster shell, that forges the pearl.

The real challenge is to create a conscious relationship. Our striking differences as men and women often have us (at the most important times!), relating to each other in ways that come across as contrary to our partners. I learned the art of sharing a message of communication that is graciously received by my partner, whilst feeling honoured and protected in my vulnerability. The most important thing is to access new ways of relating. To uncover the negative stories, you may be unconsciously carrying around about yourself, your partner and your relationship. These will be showing up energetically in how you relate and communicate. You may unknowingly be projecting your inner child's powerless story, instead of showing up in a way that aligns with the vision of love you deeply desire.

In your greatest vision of love, ask yourself, *Who am I? What kind of partner am I sharing my life with? What does our relationship look like?* Embody a new story to start to create the changes you seek. The other thing I have found challenging in maintaining trust and connection as a woman in an intimate relationship, is to stay conscious once a childhood wound has been triggered or when my feelings have been hurt. It can be difficult not to carry out childhood patterns, closing up and shutting the other out. Also, being aware of our protective and raging, wild woman inside who can awaken from slumber without warning. She comes out as our inner-protector. Often, when we need the most understanding and love from our partners, her all-encompassing nature will vehemently repel everyone away. It is most important to consciously access our feelings during this time. Underneath all these racing thoughts and fears ask yourself, *What am I feeling? Do I feel hurt, misunderstood or afraid? Am I feeling alone or unloved?* Dropping into our hearts is so hard to do when our greatest fears are turned on. However, when we express our feelings from a place of vulnerability, our partners can move towards us. They can sense their own heart through ours. They cannot connect to us emotionally through any other portal. Seeing each other's divinity first and foremost is the only way to overcome any difficult conditioning and patterns. We must meet each other from a place of wholeness.

As the Zen proverb states, "When the student is ready, the teacher will appear."[4] I have found this wisdom to be the same in reverse, "Once the teacher is ready, the student will appear." This began happening naturally in my coaching practice. I was attracting women who were stuck in difficult experiences with men. They were unable to manifest their greatest desires in love, whilst carrying out the same patterns repeatedly. Some of my clients were in relationships and marriages that lacked fulfilment, understanding and connection. I saw how much their partners and families suffered, being so out of balance.

So, as my own relationship soared to extraordinary new grounds of love and commitment, I started teaching women how to rescript their own love stories. I taught them how to drop into their powerful feminine energy. I shared practical tools to help couples reunite in harmony and resolve their heartaches. It has been beyond fulfilling and rewarding to see women so empowered, creating and receiving the love they yearn for.

I realised through all this, that I had finally broken the pattern of unsupportive and self-sacrificing relationships in my own family lineage. This was a tremendous gift I could pass down to my three beautiful daughters. Something I had previously felt so powerless to change. My deepest wish for women is for them to experience their most self-honouring vision of love, thus deeply supporting their long-term happiness and wellbeing. I am so passionate about

---

[4] TheMindsJournal.com

working with women one-to-one, in group circles and in workshops. In these formats, we are able to deep-dive into their feminine hearts, uncover their manifestation power and the divine magic within. All while reminding them, that a woman who knows she's powerful, is the most powerful woman there is!

Your Gift

Robyn is offering our readers her free PDF on How to Enhance Healthy Communication in Your Relationship, to support you to receive the emotional connection and understanding you want. It's time to stop going without, now! Please find the link in her bio on Instagram and Facebook.

www.facebook.com/robyn.chant

www.instagram.com/robyn_lovecoach

LEIGH JANE WOODGATE

There comes a time in your life when you're no longer willing to settle for anything less than that which your soul is craving for. You reach a point of ZERO tolerance for bullsh*t. And when that moment arrives, you begin to walk the path of claiming ALL of you. There is no going back! You raise your standards. Say YES to all the things and people that light you up. And NO to anything and everyone that isn't FULLY aligned with the highest version of yourself. This is empowerment.

A woman who puts herself before others in order to be of greater service to those who need her most. This is empowerment. A woman who chooses to love and care for herself in ways beyond that which any other human can love and care for her. This is empowerment. A woman who chooses to raise her frequency, elevate her level of consciousness, and become crystal clear on her purpose on planet Earth. This is empowerment.

And no matter how many distractions may be circling her orbit of magnificence, she stays true to herself, laser-focused on her mission at hand, untouchable by the external world. Empowerment does not equal invincibility. It is the epitome of unf*ckwithability.

Untriggerable. Unstoppable. Unapologetically YOU!.

Leigh Jane is a Business Growth Advisor, Leadership Mentor, Author of two #1 international bestselling books "Trailblazers" and "Awakening", and the Founder of Inategy Business School, a Leadership Collective and Online Business School that enables Conscious Leaders, Purpose-Driven Entrepreneurs, and Socially Minded Coaches, Consultants, Advisors and Healers to build and grow profitable and sustainable Multi-6-7 Figure Businesses, without having to compromise who they truly are.

Born and raised in Johannesburg, South Africa. Living, loving and serving in Sydney, Australia with her son, Noah the Kid.

www.leighjanewoodgate.com

JOERGETTE MAE MEDEL

Joergette Mae Medel is The Soul Igniter. She empowers Purpose-Driven Women to RISE and Transform their Pain into Passion, Purpose and Power, so that they can ultimately live their passions and love their life.

Her mission is to help women embody their true authentic self and remove the blocks that are holding them back from realising their true potential. As an International Speaker, Passion Coach and Intuitive Guide, Joergette integrates practical tools with spiritual practices and facilitates transformational healing journeys for her clients.

Amongst her many accolades, Joergette is a Certified Passion Test Facilitator, Heal Your Life Teacher and Art of Feminine Presence Teacher. She is also a recipient of the 'Iconic Leaders Creating a Better World for All' Award at the Annual Women Economic Forum in India 2019.

Joergette helps women come back to their hearts, embrace their shadows and shed the things which no longer serve them. She serves to remind women that they are spiritual, infinite beings having a human experience and strives to provide tools to help women live in alignment with their passions and purpose.

TRANSFORMING PAIN INTO PASSION, PURPOSE AND POWER

Have you ever felt like you were dying inside because you had lost your sense of identity? Have you ever felt as though something was missing in your life? Have you ever had the yearning to be more, do more and have more? But because you felt trapped by the fear of judgement, you felt torn to choose between your purpose and your family?

My dear sister, if you have ever felt that way, I see you. I feel you. I witness you. I have such deep compassion and reverence for you because I have also been there. I too once felt stuck and felt like I had no choice. I know what it feels like to want to move in a certain direction, but not be able to due to an unsupportive husband. I know how it feels to put everybody else's needs above my own and made to feel guilty for putting my own needs first. I too was once that woman, living my life according to other people's expectations as a woman, a wife and a mother.

I have always known and felt that I was here for a bigger purpose. I have been on my personal evolution journey for a long time. Ever since I attended my very first Breakthrough to Success seminar with Christopher Howard in 2005, I felt a deeper calling. I still remember sitting in that auditorium, excited about the fire that had been ignited deep within my soul. I wanted to spread my wings and be of service in a much bigger way. However, at the time, I was newly married. Our children were still quite young, and we were struggling financially. As much as I deeply desired to pursue my dreams, I also wanted to uphold the image of being a "good wife" and a "good mother". Being a woman, I was expected to behave in a certain way. Being a Catholic, Filipina woman took this to another level. I felt the expectations of being a loyal, Catholic, Filipino woman who always listens to, and does, whatever her husband says. A woman who sacrifices her needs and desires to serve only the needs of her family and who never prioritises herself. These expectations were all weighing on me. Every day, I was reminded to make sure I lived up to these expectations. The conditioning was embedded so deeply, and I was so scared of the tribal shame I would experience going against the grain. So instead, I went back to work full time, and put a halt on my dreams.

Over the years, I became increasingly unhappy and unfulfilled. Whilst I loved being a mum, I was dying inside. I felt so lost. I had lost my identity. I didn't know who I was anymore. My whole world had become about everybody else, and I came to realise that throughout my whole life, I was being who everyone else expected me to be. I was living the life they expected me to live. In March 2013, my world fell apart. I received a text message that would forever change the course of my life: "If you're going to follow your heart, then I'm going to follow mine. I made a mistake 6 years ago. I want a separation before you go to Dallas."

I still remember that day so vividly. It was my first day at a new job. Holding back the tears, I sat there stunned. All I could do was read those words over and over again. I didn't know how to react or how to even respond. *Could this be it?* I thought. Is it really time for this journey to end? I just sat there, frozen. For once, I was lost for words. That wasn't the first time I wanted to travel overseas in pursuit of my dreams. Only a couple of months previously in January of that same year, I went on a Leadership Cruise to Miami and Mexico, a difficult decision to make at the time. Have you ever decided to do something that seemed completely crazy and illogical, but you just knew you had to do it? Well, this was one of those moments. When I made that decision, I was met with such

146

opposition. I was forbidden to go. As I was given an ultimatum if I went on the trip: divorce.

With a heavy heart, and feeling this burden on my shoulders, I still chose to go. This was the first time in my life that I travelled on my own. I felt so free and so liberated! I learned so much about myself, and I got to meet so many beautiful souls on that trip. I had the most amazing time and I have no regrets. As I look back, I can see how this event was a pivotal moment in my life. With a renewed sense of self, I came home promising myself that I would always say yes to my heart's true desires.

So, there I was in March 2013, sitting in front of my computer. I was excited about my first day at a new job and planning my trip to Dallas. I was following my dreams, pulled towards my vision, and driven by a massive desire to make a positive impact in people's lives. But the rug was about to be pulled out from under my feet. My world as I knew it came crashing down. My husband, whom I had been with for 11 years, wanted a separation as he didn't support my vision anymore. I had grown so much, and I wanted to keep growing. Our communication had broken down. Our marriage had been torn apart. *How had we grown so far apart?* I still remember driving home that night after work. I packed whatever clothes I could fit into the car; got the kids and we drove to the only place I knew I could find some solace, my parent's house. I had nowhere else to go and no one else to turn to.

As challenging as it was, the only thing I could do was keep moving forward. I chose to stay strong, not only for me, but more importantly for my kids. I came back to the principles that I learned from my mentor, Janet Attwood, co-author of the book *The Passion Test*[5]. I felt like the universe had thrown this challenge

---

[5] Attwood, Janet & Chris (2012). The Passion Test: The effortless path to discovering your destiny. Hachette Australia.

on my path to evaluate my resolve; to really test my belief in myself and in this work; and to truly encourage me to walk my talk as a Passion Coach and Certified Passion Test Facilitator. One of the biggest principles I learned from my mentor Janet Attwood, is the formula for living a passionate life. I learned this from the book *The Passion Test* and it has made such a tremendous impact in my life. So much so, that I still live by these principles today. The formula is simply this - intention, attention, no tension.

Everything starts with intention. Intention is about getting absolute clarity on what you desire to create in your life. It's about getting clear on what's truly important to you. There's a beautiful quote from *The Passion Test* [6] that has stuck in my mind to this very day. It sums up the importance of intention: "When you are clear, what you want will show up in your life, and only to the extent that you're clear." Having clarity is important, however it isn't enough. You can have the best intentions, but if you never act towards them, nothing happens. This is where attention comes in. Once you are clear of your intentions, the second step is to place your attention on them. It's time to take inspired action to help manifest this into reality. When taking action, it's important to make sure you place your attention only on what is working and not dwell on what isn't working. Stay positive and focus only on the things you can control.

What does this look like in real life? In my workshops and one-on-one sessions with clients, I always share this classic example. Let's say that your intention is to have a better relationship with money. What happens when you get an electricity bill? Is your automatic response, "Oh my God, how expensive is this?" or "How are we going to pay for this?" or maybe, "I can't freaking afford this"? Or is it something like: "Oh my God, thank you so much electricity company," because this means that you were able to use the heater to keep your family

---

[6] Groover, R J (2013). The Art of Feminine Presence Teacher Training. Melbourne, Australia.

warm this winter? "This means that we were able to watch Netflix and keep the family entertained." Or, similarly, "This means that we were able to use the internet and computer to keep our business operating." Are you focusing on the gratitude for what you were able to receive because of that bill? Or are you focusing on the negatives, the scarcity and the fear of lack? Because they are vastly different energies.

Now that you have clarity on your intentions, and you have started placing your attention on taking inspired action, the third step is no tension. This part is the trickiest part for most people because it's all around letting go and surrendering to the process. Getting clear and taking inspired action towards the things you desire are easy. But, when it's time to let go and detach, it can be extremely challenging. The reason it's the trickiest part is that as humans, we like to have a sense of control. We can be very impatient, and we want things to happen instantaneously. We like to control how they happen and when they happen. When things don't go our way or according to plan, we tighten the grip on our expectations. We get angry and we even project blame onto other people.

When this happens, it can be incredibly challenging to be in a place of calm. The quickest way I know how to get back into a state of peace is through gratitude. Come back to an *Attitude of Gratitude* by placing your attention on all the things you can be grateful for in that moment, however big or small. Once you're in a state of peace and calm, you can begin to place your absolute trust and faith in the universe, God, or whatever higher power you resonate with. Have faith and surrender. Whatever you are desiring to manifest, whatever you are calling in - your intentions, your goals, whatever it is - trust that it's going to be delivered to you in perfect divine timing, and in the way that is perfect just for you. Get clear, take inspired action and then, let go.

When you let go and let God, it allows you to be at peace. When you're in a place of calm, you become centred. It is in this state of peace and calm where magic and miracles can start to occur. You create a vacuum and attract the things, people, opportunities, circumstances, and synchronicities that help manifest your intentions and bring them into your physical reality. With this formula, I chose to dive deeper into my passions. Using *The Passion Test*, I got clear on my top five passions. I pursued the things that brought me joy and pleasure and I started to notice the magic that was unfolding in my life. I noticed that when I started doing the things I loved, life started to become so much brighter and clearer. Driven by my insatiable hunger to learn, I attended seminars and workshops again. I started attracting like-minded friends and like-hearted souls. I got back in touch with my femininity. As I started doing the practices I learned from my *Art of Feminine Presence [2]* teacher training, I started to harmonise my inner masculine and inner feminine aspects.

I gained even more clarity on the life I wanted to create and the intimate partnership I desired to have. I practised self-love and gratitude daily. I just kept focusing on having fun and experiencing joy and pleasure each day. I even started salsa dance classes, and that's where I eventually met my soulmate. Fast forward to now, I have an amazing soulful partnership with my twin flame. Along with both our beautiful twin girls and my older kids, we have created a beautiful family together. After all these years, I never stopped dreaming. I held on to my vision of being able to have it all - to live my passions and purpose whilst being an amazing partner and mother. Being a mum to four beautiful children, my journey has not been easy. I have experienced the highest of highs and the lowest of lows throughout this rollercoaster ride of life. I had to die a thousand times to be able to rise from the ashes and fully claim my calling. And just as the Phoenix rises from the ashes, I too have clawed my way through the dark, risen through the challenges and obstacles I have faced only to be reborn multiple times over.

I continue to be tested and it's not always easy to stay positive all the time. Each time I decide to say yes to my dreams, I am met with challenges and obstacles along the way. A perfect example of this is when I decided to pursue an international speaking opportunity in India and speak at the *Women Economic Forum* in April 2019. My family were not in the best financial situation. I was working full time in a demanding job at the time, so it was challenging to take time off work. With all the obstacles on my path, it was hard to find a way. I felt deep in my core that I was meant to speak at that event, but I had no idea how I was going to make it happen. I was being called to lean into the resistance. I was being called to be creative and to think outside the box. Most importantly, I was being called to trust and surrender to the process; to let go and *Let God.*

Once again, I turned to the principles I learned from my mentor. Using the formula of intention, attention, no tension, the universe guided me to India. There I was able to fulfil my dream of becoming an international speaker and recipient of the *Iconic Leaders Creating a Better World for All Award.* In February 2020, I fulfilled another dream of empowering women in the Philippines, where I was invited to speak at the *Leading with Heart: Global Women's Summit* in Manila. What was even more miraculous was that I was able to make it back home safely just before borders started closing due to COVID-19. The more I choose to say yes to my dreams and practice that simple formula of intention, attention, no tension, more magic and miracles continue to happen in my life. Because of this, I live each day now with a grateful heart, embracing all of life's perfect imperfections. I see things differently. I feel differently. I act differently. I have full faith and trust that I am always guided by the universe. My job in co-creating the life I desire is to have absolute clarity on what I genuinely want and to get out of my own way, to let the universe show me the path, be patient and surrender to the process. This is not the easiest path to travel, but it's well worth it.

I choose to believe that there is a purpose for everything that happens in our life. When seemingly negative things occur, you always have a choice. You can choose for that crisis to break you; or you can choose to have that crisis be the catalyst for your transformation. It is always your choice. Whilst my life is far from being picture-perfect, I get to enjoy my life with my amazing partner who supports me unconditionally. He sees me and loves me for who I truly am. I get to be a mum to my gorgeous kids, and I get to be *me* without compromising my values. Together as a family, we are striving towards consciously creating our dream life.

I've been through the struggles. I've been through the heartaches. I have been torn apart. This is why I'm so enthusiastic about sharing my story and helping women step into their truth and share it without shame. I'm on a mission to help women embody their true authentic self and remove the blocks that are holding them back from realising their true potential. So, let me ask you - what if you didn't have to choose? What if there was a way for you to live your purpose and enjoy your family? Imagine for a moment what it would be like to be living your passions, doing the things you love and living your purpose. Imagine experiencing a loving, passionate, intimate relationship with your partner, whilst still being an amazing mother and inspirational role model to your children? Well sister, I'm here to tell you that it is not only possible; it is your absolute birthright! You don't have to choose. You can live your purpose *and* enjoy your family. Allow me to show you how.

I've journeyed through many adversities in my life. I've gone through some challenging times and I've had to face my darkest shadows as well as my deepest fears. What I've come to realise and truly believe is that each crisis was an initiation that became the catalyst to my transformation.

Your Gift

To express Joergette's deepest gratitude and appreciation to those who have taken the time to share in her journey and her story, Joergette would love to gift you with her video series called 4 steps to RISE — How to Transform your Pain into Passion, Purpose and Power you can find the series at www.joergettemaemedel.com/rise

www.joergettemaemedel.com
www.facebook.com/JoergetteMaeMedel
www.instagram.com/joergettemaemedel

"And the day came when the risk to remain tight in a bud was more painful than the risk it took to blossom."

~ Anaïs Nin

TAMMIE PIKE

Wyrd Smith, Speaker, & Business Creative, Tammie is dedicated to helping women to unlock their magic within to become the woman they desire to be in life and in business. A born-and-raised small town country girl with nothing more than passion, purpose, and a dream to empower women worldwide, Tammie is proud to have helped hundreds of women share their stories, gifts, services and messages through the written and spoken word on her different platforms, that have reached hundreds of thousands of people worldwide.

Seeking new ways to share her gifts and knowledge, Tammie lets her curiosity, intuition and creativity lead the way from speaking on stage in India, publishing a worldwide digital magazine, writing, publishing books, interviewing, creating and facilitating at retreats, including alongside her favourite author of Eat Pray Love, Elizabeth Gilbert in Fiji.

Empowerment Is A
Never Ending Journey

What does it mean to embark on a journey to empowerment? Or even simpler, what does 'empowerment' mean? I believe empowerment is very individual to each woman, and like with any self-development, there is never an end destination where you are simply 'empowered'. Empowerment is a continuous journey, one that has many layers, stops, and detours. It starts in the little moments, the choices and actions you take, such as when you say 'yes' to yourself, or 'no' to others, and when you stand up and share your opinion. It's when you rally for those who need help or don't have a voice or resources at their disposal. It's about making decisions based on what is suitable for you and not what others tell you to do. It's about not seeking approval from others, knowing it's okay if someone doesn't agree with you or like you. You aren't everyone's cup of tea and not everyone is yours, and that's perfectly fine! This is you taking your power back as it has always been yours.

I believe empowerment is when you seek your own answers by doing your own research, as well as being discerning where you seek your information and what you take on. To gain knowledge is to gain power; however, we need the right knowledge, knowledge that we don't generally find in conventional or social media, you need to look beyond. Once you gain that knowledge, you have the power to share it with others, even if it goes against the 'norm'. Empowerment is about giving yourself permission to be different and to honour that you are different, to find a place for those quirks, gifts, and unique ideas to flourish, rather than shutting them down.

The knowledge you are seeking is what you need within your life. There are many places you can find this knowledge. For instance, if you have been told to take a certain medication yet it feels wrong, get a second or even a third opinion.

Do your research, ask lots of questions, seek alternative options if they are available. You don't need to settle, if you know that it doesn't feel right. Or, it could be that you are in a toxic relationship and feel unworthy, unconfident, or unsafe to leave because you don't have support or know what rights or options you have. However, if you are able to research, you can gain knowledge and find the right support, information, and laws that can help protect you and support you should you decide to leave.

I learned that knowledge can dramatically impact those around you. In 2014 my youngest daughter, Brookie, was born. We found out early on that she had a dual-chamber kidney with two ureters that weren't connected properly to her bladder. This led to a kidney infection at seven weeks, where she experienced fibril convulsions and stopped breathing. We spent a week in the hospital. We both experienced trauma, and that situation led me to experience extreme anxiety and panic attacks constantly, as I thought I would lose her every time she was unwell. But this was only the start of her health crisis, and she would continue to have UTI (Urinary Tract Infection) after UTI. She was an unwell baby and lived on me 24/7 for the first six months.

When we were in hospital the first time, the doctors prescribed half a dose of antibiotics daily until she was eighteen months old to try and reduce the recurrence of the UTI's. Deep within me, I knew this was wrong, but when I voiced my concerns, they said it was their protocol and the only thing they could prescribe. I knew there had to be another way, but what? Thankfully, one student paediatrician told me on the third night in the hospital to go and research probiotics and the studies that were done in America on the effectiveness of probiotics versus antibiotics for continued use. So I did. I have never been more thankful to technology or my smart phone. I researched day and night, as I couldn't sleep in hospital anyway, but researching alternative and holistic ways to heal my daughter quickly became my obsession. When we went home, I would eagerly get up to Brookie during the night for her feedings, or to help her settle, just so I could research more. (I researched so much that I got RSI (Repetitive Strain Injury) in my thumbs from scrolling so much!) The more knowledge I gained, the more clarity I had, and the more confident I became in my belief that there were alternative ways. I took my research to Brookie's doctors, and they couldn't dispute it. In fact, they knew about it, but they weren't allowed to go down that path because it wasn't protocol. I became so confident in the path I was to take, that even though my husband, some family members, and friends were unsupportive of my decision, I did it anyway. Those friends are no longer in my circle and my heart still aches sometimes for the loss, but it was a time in my life that showed me my inner strength, my resilience and ability to believe in myself, and the knowledge I had. It took a truck load of courage to ignore the naysayers, especially since they were major influences in my life.

Another time when knowledge gave me power, clarity, confidence, and courage was in our business when we had a difficult client who wouldn't pay a substantial bill. We went down the normal paths of recovering the debt, but the customer became abusive and threatening. I took action; I did my research. I reached out for legal advice and was able to take the matter to court, where the judges quickly sided with us. It took us nearly nine months to recover our items, but it was worth it as it gave me more confidence in my ability to protect our business and to know our rights.

Then, a few years ago I was given yet another challenge or should I say lessons. My horse, RM, a beautiful Morgan, had a major paddock injury that caused septic arthritis in his hock (knee) that led to two major surgeries. But because the infection was still there, one of the vets made the decision that my horse needed to be put down. Again, I *felt* what the right thing to do was and I knew that I could help him to get better. I did my research on what had helped other horses with similar injuries. I also reached out to others who had similar experiences and heard what worked for them. I became confident in my knowledge. I then had the courage to go against the vet's decision. I got my horse float and picked up RM, and as I was about to leave, the vet rang me and told me I was making the wrong decision and that I was putting him through unnecessary pain, as he would have to be put down soon anyway. I thanked him for his concern and told him I would manage. It was an extremely difficult and challenging time. However, RM wanted to live; I felt it in my bones. So, I did everything to help him. It took nearly six months to clear the infection and even longer to get him sound. Yet, RM is now galloping around in our paddock, and happy to be alive!

Earlier this year, I was given an opportunity to purchase a horse that I had loved afar for sixteen years and dreamed of having in my paddock. As soon as he arrived, I knew something was wrong, I felt it and told my eldest daughter. It was little things at first. Then, as I spent more time with him, it became even more obvious that there were some serious underlying issues though not easily seen. This time I sought out three professionals who were able to work on him and diagnose multiple health issues. Within three weeks of having him, I made the hard call, one that had kept me up many nights and made me physically ill, of having to put him down. However, I had confidence in the knowledge I had gained, and that backed up the feeling I had. It was an extremely emotional time for us and the previous owner, but once it was over, and he was in a place of peace with no pain, I felt a calm come over me especially when the vet yet again confirmed he did indeed have many health issues.

There have been many instances where I have empowered myself with knowledge and listened to my intuition. My instinct is to question everything especially when I am told to ask none, maybe it's the rebel within me, yet, it has never led me astray. We have a right to ask, we have a right to be curious and to find the truth. When fear is rampant, and runs wild within, the first thing to do is take your power back by gaining knowledge, it will steady you as you gain clarity and confidence in what steps to take.

Researching and gaining knowledge has helped me grow multiple businesses, and create a unique lifestyle for our family and myself. I have been able to help others due to my ability to be resourceful, responsible, and independent in my thinking and the choices I am willing to make based on the confidence I have to question the status quo. I'm not suggesting that you don't listen to your doctor or professionals. What I am suggesting to you is that it's okay to question. It's okay to follow that inner 'knowing' when something doesn't feel quite right with something that you have been told. Do your own research and find other people who can help and support you to find the answers that you are seeking. The most important part is not to stick your head in the sand and to be brave enough to open yourself to the truth, as sometimes the truth can be scary and not what we want to hear. Yet it will empower us in the end.

I believe that knowledge can create clarity, clarity can create confidence, and confidence can build courage that enables you to take the next step whether it's in your life, family, business, workplace, or community.

When I first started my journey of self-discovery and personal development, it was really uncomfortable, not only for me, but especially for my husband, Nathan. One day, he had a Betty Crocker wife who did everything to make his life easier and whose main aim was to please him, giving all of my love, energy, and body to do so. But after experiencing a breakdown that led me to my breakthrough after Brookie's health crisis, I knew I had to change. I knew it was time to stop being the person everyone else wanted me to be, and to be who I truly was. It was difficult, as I couldn't research on the internet or in books to find out who I was, what I needed, or what I wanted. That was an internal job. So, I embarked on my healing journey through alternative modalities, seeking mentors and teachers who could help me find my way back to myself. Layer by layer, I started uncovering the diamond within. Instead of self-loathing, I found self-love and self-belief in a woman that was strong, kind, and resilient. A woman who had overcome many of life's challenges. Yes, she had wounds, but she could still see the magic in the world around her also. I leaned into that. It awakened a gift of speaking. I deepened my intuition. I focused on my strengths and built upon my weaknesses. I delved and revelled in my spirituality and all things mystical. It brought me so much joy, but it brought my husband so much fear. To be honest, he was a muggle who saw life in black and white, and as his wife (I had always hidden my light and anything to do with spirituality and emotions) was now a multicoloured, spiritual and honest-speaking woman.

And it scared him. It pushed against everything he knew to be true. It challenged his beliefs, and more than anything, it made him uncomfortable. One day, after going to a spiritual festival and listening to some incredible speakers, I came home and shared the new revelations I had about myself with him. I was on a natural high and told him about the changes I was going to make, and he saw, yet again, his wife changing. He asked me: "When is everything going to go back to normal?" I knew his 'normal' meant him having a 'normal' wife who did 'normal' things, things that to me represented a woman I used to be, where I was unhappy and would give everything to everyone else to make them happy but was dying inside. Yet, no one knew because I plastered a smile on my face and acted like a super woman who could do it all, when in all truth, I was falling to pieces and failing hard.

My newfound confidence and self-belief I had been gaining as I uncovered more about myself, gave me the courage to tell my husband: "I love myself too much to ever go back to the woman I was". I told him the truth about how I felt, that I was dying inside, pretending to be someone I wasn't. Then I said to him, with utter love in my heart: "I know who I am today isn't the woman you married, and I know you want the Betty Crocker type wife, so if you are unhappy, I want you to know that you can leave and find a woman you want because I'm going to keep growing and changing". We both cried and it was hard, but Nathan looked at me and said: "I love you and I want to be with you". That was six years ago, and it hasn't been an easy road, there have been times when he has got scared and tried to stop my growth because it challenged his beliefs and comfort zone. Each time I would say: "I am never going to stop growing and changing. You are welcome to come with me, or you are welcome to stay and let me go". And each time he stayed. We have grown into a partnership that is mutually supportive, loving, as well as being honest and keeping each other in check (when we need it), but we know our strengths and our weaknesses, and we don't pretend to be something we're not for the sake of pleasing one another. We have now been together twenty years and I can honestly say that it keeps getting better and better and I don't regret a single decision I made, nor the actions I've taken that empowered me in my life.

For me, being empowered is also being willing to move through your fear and step out of your comfort zone. How many times have you heard 'Life begins at the end of your comfort zone?'

Some ways to start stepping out of your comfort zone might be doing simple things such as changing your daily routine, wearing your 'special' clothes just because, buy yourself something special, take time out without guilt or you might want to stretch yourself with talking to a stranger, learn a new skill, have difficult conversations in a loving way, apply for your dream job, face one of your fears and on the list goes.

With growth, self-care must come and most importantly implementing practices that bring you back to your centre. For me, it's my morning walk, where I become present, looking at the beauty and magic in my surroundings, and listening to the birds and other creatures, while I speak my gratitude and partake in my daily rituals of cleansing and clearing my energy. Another practice that helps me to find my calm each day, and I invite you to give it a go even though it might sound strange, is that I see myself as a tree (you can see yourself as any tree, for me it's a coconut tree). My tree has deep, strong roots, grounded into the earth, roots that can weather any storm, that can grow in the harshest of conditions and still thrive. It doesn't let what's going on around it influence it, change it, or hinder it. It only offers what is natural for it to produce (coconuts). It provides shade to others without having to give all of itself to do so. It's simply a coconut tree, and everyone acknowledges this and understands its ability. I see these qualities and I remind myself of who I am and what I naturally offer and the boundaries I need to enforce so I don't overgive or get into people-pleasing, giving what I don't have to give. I can tell you, if I don't do this each morning, I can easily get off balance that then affects the rest of my day and those around me; it's simple, yet effective.

I also invite you to start following your inner and outer signs. If you get a feeling, thought, idea, or dream over and over again, lean into it. Explore it with curiosity. Journal it or talk about it with someone. For instance, in my darkest time, I needed something more to help me through, where everything seemed too hard and too much. I started being more aware of the signs around me, which is when I started seeing recurring numbers. I talked to my psychic friend about them, she told me they are called 'angel numbers'. The numbers would appear on a clock, an odometer, on barcodes, bank statements, phone numbers, and so I started to… research it, (you got it) and the message the numbers represented became a reassurance, especially when I had a feeling or persistent idea, it would back it up. Then it became a conversation with the universe, and one I still have to this day because even though I have strengthened my intuition, I am human and still experience doubt and times of emotional turmoil, and they are always there if I am open to see and willing to listen.

I also love seeing the synchronicities (not just with numbers) within life and the experiences I have had; I have so many I could write a book. "A synchronicity is a series of events where something other than the probability of chance is involved, and this it feels meaningful". "It is an event where needs are met, people are encountered, or things just come together perfectly when we need them." says Monica Berg, author and co-host of the Spiritually Hungry Podcast.

For example, you might talk about someone you haven't seen for a long time and all of a sudden, they reach out to you. You might dream of a koala and then you start seeing them everywhere (look up spirit animals). One of my most incredible experiences started out when the book Eat Pray Love written by Elizabeth Gilbert fell off a shelf at an Airbnb I was staying at, took me on a journey of epic proportions and experiences from Melbourne, Bali and India, to becoming a retreat facilitator beside Elizabeth Gilbert at Liesel Albrecht's famous Ultimate Girls Week Away in Fiji in 2020. (But that is a story for another day.) I think, though, that by seeing the synchronicities within life, it opens you up to see other magical things within your life.

Lastly, I love channelled writing as another empowering practice, and I invite you to be playful with it because if it's your first time learning about this, you might feel silly when giving it a go. Channelled writing (for me) is when you write down a question and then ask yourself, your higher self, God or your spiritual entity to share with you what it is you need to know for your highest potential. Then, you simply write without thinking, judging, or pausing. I have been doing this for years and have over twenty plus books of channelled writing. It has given me so much clarity, reassurance, and some really great advice, content, and confidence. Whether you believe it or not, give it a go! You just might be surprised by what you find.

I think the key to anything in life is to try to not take everything too seriously, to have fun, to play and be curious and willing to try different things. I continue to work on this within myself, as I can be very critical with everything I do and miss the joy in what I am doing. I am getting better, but I lapse every now and again. As I tell others, we are only human and being a human is accepting you can't be perfect.

Your Gift

Tammie's gift to you is to offer a free self-awareness DIY coaching session, and an eBook on How to Own and Write Your Story that you can download off her website. Both of these offers will help you to grow your self-awareness, give you clarity, and help you build your confidence, so you have the courage to be you and to share your story to empower others. Enjoy!

www.Empoweredpublishing.com.au

www.facebook.com/empoweredpublishing

Bek Tomarchio

Bek Tomarchio was a free and loving spirit. She was happiest in nature, dancing, in conscious conversation, or creating magic with her sisters Belinda and Katie. Bek was an Intuitive Guide who used art to foster connection and care of the feminine essence and for a future of divinely aligned women. She was a Yoni Essence artist; her sacred art is deeply imbued with unconditional love and intuitive alchemy. She was also a warrior of love, and her wish was to leave a legacy for our world to be where death is not feared, and your truth is never ignored.

LIVE LIKE THERE IS NO TOMORROW

Death. So many people fear it. And they let this fear prevent them from doing the things they want to do. But what if you were told, today, that your days were numbered? Would you change the way you live your life?

This is not the story of life. This is not the story of death. Instead, this is a story of how to live as though you were dying. Because if you are living your authentic life, if you are showing up as your authentic self every day, then the way you live now will be no different than the way you live when you know death is knocking.

This is what Bek Tomarchio has taught us; this is her message, powerful and strong. "Life is too fucking short. And all we have is this present moment. It's ALL that we have."

So, what are you doing with your present moment?

Bek's story of self-transformation has a happy ending, but it is not the happy ending you would expect. She did not live 'happily ever after.' Instead, her happy ending is in how voraciously she lived and loved, how gracefully and confidently she met with death, and how profound and beautiful the legacy she leaves behind is.

I believe her story will activate you in such a powerful way that its message will last a lifetime.

So, as Bek would say, it's time to "get down in there." It's time to get "spiritually fierce."

Bek had her fair share of trials and tribulations throughout her life. A traumatic childhood, a toxic job, a breakdown, and a diagnosis of PTSD were all hurdles Bek faced in her quest for transformation. But this story is not about her past pain or her traumas; it's about how she overcame them and found the path to

167

living her very best life. When Bek left teaching, she began her path of healing. Bek invested in her personal and spiritual development through a spiritual course that helped her break through many of her limiting beliefs and layers of trauma. It wasn't an easy path to take, yet like with anything Bek did, she went all in and gave her everything. Of course, she stumbled many times, but each time she just got up, dusted herself off, and took the next step into her next day. Bek never gave up and never wavered from her path of becoming spiritually fierce. She was mentally focused on living a life she knew she wanted and deserved; she was determined to live life to the fullest.

This led to her most powerful work. Bek was able to overcome the fear of dying, and her work shares her extraordinary journey. It is a very unexplored realm, a taboo topic at times — death. It isn't something we, as a society, talk openly about. But Bek did. She did the things we 'aren't supposed to do when faced with death.' She spoke about it. She laughed about it. She accepted it. She embraced it. Her grace and humour sliced right through it as though facing death were the most natural thing in the world.

When Bek was diagnosed with a rare uterine tumour, she overcame her fear of the unknown while traversing the pain of her diagnosis. She did not meet the news with rage and denial; instead, she faced it with wisdom, grace, and an acceptance that her sisters and mother, Debby, will never forget. Bek gave her life to the sacredness that is God/Universal Energy/Source/The All. Her story is full of wisdom that she openly and graciously shared with the world so that we can all learn, grow, and evolve. She challenges us to step out of fear and into the joy and power that comes from truly living our life.

In an extraordinary interview with Ricci-Jane Adams, the principal and creator of The Institute for Intuitive Intelligence, with whom Bek studied to become a Third-Level Priestess. Bek shared her wisdom and enlightenment. She had this conversation with only days left on this earth plane, and her laughter and strength were astounding. She is in, what should be, her darkest hour, yet, she shines so brightly. She is clearly not afraid of death; on the contrary, she emanates grace. She is radiant throughout the conversation, humble but unapologetic. And it is evident, right from the very first word, that she wants you to find the same happiness that she has found. She implores you to remove your mask and to embrace your authentic self, to detonate love bombs all around you, and to 'unfuck' yourself, as she has.

As Bek jumps right into her interview, she shares that her journey of the end of her life hadn't been easy. It took a lot of work to meet her shadow and the fears that lay within. Yes, she did, and she invites us to do the same.

Bek openly shares that the love of her sisters, Belinda & Katie, and the love of her sisterhood, helped her immensely throughout her life, especially during her final journey. "The importance of a sisterhood is that they support you when you think you can't possibly keep going; they will hold you and help you through it," Bek stated.

Many people, however, don't have a sisterhood or support system. Is it because they think they don't need it, or is it more because they feel unworthy? When we feel unworthy, that's when the spiritual and inner work comes in. That's where we take the time to heal our inner child, trauma, limiting beliefs and programming, where we ultimately let go of the belief of being unworthy of love. Isn't that what it comes down to? Not feeling worthy of being loved and feeling loved? Bek is a testament to what life can be like when we do the inner work and what living a wholehearted life can feel like.

With her voice filled with joy, Bek shared: "Allow love in, to experience unconditional love in every way, shape or form. It is here, and it is everywhere, even more so in the time of turmoil and heartbreaks."

Bek, in the conversation, is also passionate about people seeking support for whatever they are going through, and it doesn't take much to find it. "You only have to seek it [support], ask for it, and it will be yours," shared Bek. There are people, organisations, charities, professionals (and the list goes on) willing and waiting to help you.

Nothing can prepare you for death; it is painful saying goodbye to loved ones. But, as Bek expresses, the journey of dying can also be the most beautiful and blessed experience. Not fearing death allows you to see the beauty and majesticness of feeling the connection to 'the one'. As Bek says, when you 'look at a sunset, you become immersed in this majestic-ness. You feel 'God/The One/Universal Energy'; you feel that connection." There is grace in letting go of all attachments to this life. Our life is a gift. One day, we are present, and the next, we are not. Bek talks about death without fear, without trepidation. When she talks about what she believes death will be like, she offers these eloquent and powerful words: "I'm just going to be, and then I'm just not going to be".

This isn't to say Bek wanted to leave this earth plane. She wanted more than anything to keep living. At 41, Bek felt she had finally created her dream life. She had finally unfucked herself and had finally become who she was always meant to be. One of Bek's gifts that was awakened in the last couple of years of her life was becoming a sensual artist. Bek found her passion, her voice. After years of suppressing her needs and desires for the sake of approval and fitting in, she was finally able to articulate precisely what she wanted. She knew how she wanted to live her life, especially as she knew this particular journey was coming to an end.

When Bek was diagnosed with only six weeks to live, there weren't many changes that she made within her life. This is a testament to the life she was already living. Bek was already enjoying every day, living each day to the fullest. She was surrounded by the people she loved, living in her dream home with her beloved partner, Chris. Bek had already done most of the things she wanted to do and experience in this life, so when she was confronted by the fact that her days were numbered, she didn't feel the need to make any changes because she was already happy in her life. This is one of the most powerful lessons and messages that Bek leaves, to create a life that brings you so much joy that when the time comes for you to leave this life, you can leave it in a state of happiness, love, and utter contentment.

Bek had created her dream life by having boundaries, which she believed was essential because it led to living a life with no regrets. Bek believed that you shouldn't spend time with people you don't want to and shouldn't waste time doing things that are not aligned with you. Bek confidently stated, "You have a choice; whatever the options are, we can continually choose. Life is too fucking short, and all we have is this present moment." So, choose wisely. It was Bek's hope for others not to wait until something cataclysmic happens to change their lives; instead, she invites us to live our truth and do it now.

It took Bek years of consciously creating her life, slowing down, and working out what she wanted to feel and experience with her time. She lived in a way she never dreamed she could; this is all because she listened to her soul's guiding whispers.

Bek believes the key to living your best dream life is to take the time (and it might take a lot of time) to uncover how you truly want to feel, as she believed that feeling is the language the universe hears.

"Life is so short, yet there is no need to rush it," Bek shares wisely. This is not easy to achieve, especially in the society we currently live in and the programming we have brought into. It means taking time to know who you are. This might mean embarking on a healing journey to remove the layers of hurt, trauma, and conditioning of past people and experiences. It's not an easy process, yet it is one you will never regret, as each step of your journey leads you back to 'you', back to the truth of who you are.

To achieve the life we want means: "To live each day with conscious intention and in alignment with that moment, regardless of what that moment looks like. To be here, with what we have, and with who you have in front of and beside us," Bek wisely revealed.

But it is more than that. It is also knowing that living your dream life isn't about having lots of money, material things, or being famous. Living your dream life can be as simple as doing what you love. It's about creating practices that help you feel good and bring more sacredness into your everyday. Bek loved her daily rituals and recommended daily gratitude and checking in with your body. She also loved nature and recognised both its beauty and its power. She suggested going outside every day to connect with nature, to feel the sun, to listen to the sounds and to become present within your body. And every day, come back to your heart by practising Heart Coherence. Bek stated, "If your practice changes from one day to another, that's okay! As long as you are devoted to you, that's all that matters."

During their conversation, Ricci-Jane beautifully gives space for Bek to share her journey and wisdom. But when Ricci-Jane asked Bek the inevitable question, "What do you want us to know?", Bek gave us some of the most beautiful, inspirational, and powerful advice. Her answer to Ricci-Jane's question is her legacy, as these words come directly from a person who has 'walked the walk' and has achieved what so many of us hope to achieve: happiness, acceptance of one's self, unconditional love, and peace.

BEK'S FINAL MESSAGES

BE YOU, UNAPOLOGETICALLY YOU".

"Just be you," she says. "Just be unapologetically you in each moment, no matter what that looks like. Become your own best friend, learn your own language, dude. You know, I've been sleeping with my teddy bear. Who would have thought it, but I pulled out my teddy bear. About a year ago, I was doing some inner child work. I made a cubby. I followed whatever was present for me. Just gift yourself, yourself."

DO THE WORK AND EMBRACE YOUR SHADOW

"There's nothing in your shadows that is too fucking dark. Seriously, as women, as human beings, we are so goddamn resilient. We are so extraordinary. And until you have the opportunity to see that, get down in there {in your shadows} and get spiritually fierce," Bek passionately stated.

DEATH IS PART OF LIFE, SO ACCEPT IT

As shared earlier, Bek wanted to make death less taboo as she shared, "I mean, [death] it's just something that's not really talked about. It's not something that's really, I think, embraced as a culture, and it's something that happens to all of us. It's something that once the person dies and they're on the other side, your grief is like an internal injury in that you don't see it. But grief lingers; it is something that keeps affecting. So if we can, be part of creating a culture that speaks more about this. Everyone's gone through death. Everyone is going to go through it; everyone has lost someone. Everyone is gonna lose someone, so let's make it just as much as a conversation of joy."

Be you. Face yourself, your shadows, your past because there is nothing too dark. We are all beautiful. Allow yourself to see your own beauty, to feel your own resilience. And allow death to be a part of your life, a part of your conversation, a part of your joy. This is what Bek wanted us to know, and this message resonates and reverberates and will continue to do so because it is so real, so profound, so raw, and so powerful.

The interview in which Bek shared her story was done on January 8th, 2020. Just one short week later, Bek passed away. In a very intimate setting, she passed the way she wanted with her two loving sisters holding her hand. Her loss was felt by many. But her vibrance, her authenticity, and her love lives on.

"Go forth, dear ones, and embrace your own unique self. Dare to be seen in your true gloriousness. My wish for you and all women is that may you always know the shine of your magnificence, and may you find the courage and grace to shine that glow, sharing your essence openly with the world." ~ Bek Tomarchio, Spiritually Fierce magazine.

To view Bek's work and art, you can go to:

facebook.com/Intuitive-Alchemy-with-Bek-Tomarchio

Instagram.com/intuitivealchemy.sacredart

A PERSONAL NOTE FROM TAMMIE.

I want to thank Bek's sisters, Belinda and Katie, for allowing me to share her story and to Bek for saying yes in the first place. These three sisters shared a special, unique bond. They created magic in every moment they had together, and wherever they went, their powerful and loving presence was felt. In speaking with Belinda and Katie only weeks after Bek's passing, I saw how hard it was for them to witness Bek's final journey, talk about her life with me, and read and approve this chapter when their grief is still so deep with their loss. The silver lining within the grief is sharing their love and the magic that was their sister.

I would also like to thank Ricci-Jane Adams from the Institute of Intuitive Intelligence for allowing me to use content from Bek's final interview.

The world lost a bright, loving and powerful being when Bek passed. Her words and advice needs to be shared. She had such a unique take on life and death, and I really believe her words and wisdom can and will inspire many in their own lives. And this is how she lives on — by publishing her words; her legacy lives on; she is reborn again every time a new reader meets her and every time a new woman finds her message.

This chapter was a collaboration between Tammie Pike, Belinda & Katie Tomarchio and Janelle Shields.

AFTERWORD

Whatever you do, and whatever paths you decide to take, I don't believe we should make our primary goal to be empowered. Instead, let it be an ingredient to a recipe that you can create to live a life that you love. I say this as a precaution because, like with anything, you can go to extremes that can be just as detrimental as being disempowered. You can become unbalanced, overwhelmed and possibly hurt others by focusing solely on becoming empowered as an outcome instead of building on it. It will take time.

Like the women within this book, you are just as powerful, resilient, capable and strong; even if you don't feel it right now, you are. You must remember this, especially when life seems too hard, or whatever obstacle you face seems too big, you can get through it. And you don't' have to do it alone. Make sure you reach out for support. Like I tell my children, it only takes a conversation to shift your perspective, especially when that conversation is with someone who understands you and what you are experiencing, like one of the authors perhaps. The women in this book won't judge or look down upon you; rather, they are here to support you, coach you, and help you to open your mind and heart, so you can see your situation in a way that you can feel more empowered. They are women like you who are using their past experiences to help others, and that's why they are so good at what they do because they have lived it.

So, use this book to serve you as a guide, to help you find your way back to your truth. Allow each woman who has shared her story within these pages to give you hope and courage as you navigate your life's journey. Knowing that you do not need to let your past define your future or stop you from changing and growing into a different woman from who you are right now. Instead, let it empower your future with all you have learned and experienced so you can become that woman who knows her worth. Who is willing to fight for her sovereignty and of those around her. A woman who knows it is her birthright to be wild, sensual, feminine, creative, loving, and showing up in the world in whatever way feels right. A woman who loves and honours herself, for many, that woman seems impossible, yet she is within all of us; she is waiting for you to remember that you are her, and she is you. You, an empowered woman, so take back your power, stand up for what you believe in, speak and live your truth authentically and honestly so you can become the woman you most want to be and live a life you are proud of.

Remember, much like a delicate flower, you cannot rush to blossom or to be an empowered woman, nor can you rush your healing or your life, so, instead, slow down and enjoy the journey that is your life and your path to empowerment.

Until next time, keep true to you.

Much love,

Tammie Pike

Ready to share your story?

EMPOWERED

PUBLISHING

Empowering Women to Empower

www.empoweredpublising.com.au